THE MAKING OF THE MOVIE

WRITTEN BY TRACEY MILLER-ZARNEKE

CONTENTS

4–5	Foreword
6–17	Timeline
18–19	**Locations**
20–29	Wayne Manor
30–39	The Batcave
40–49	Gotham City
50–53	GCPD Building
54–55	City Hall
56–59	Energy Facility
60–61	Orphanage
62–69	Arkham Asylum
70–71	Fortress of Solitude
72–75	Phantom Zone
76–77	**Characters**
78–87	Batman
88–91	Bruce Wayne
92–95	Alfred Pennyworth

96–99	Barbara Gordon
100–101	Batgirl
102–105	Jim Gordon
106–109	Dick Grayson
110–111	Robin
112–119	The Joker
120–127	Harley Quinn
128–131	Catwoman
132–133	The Riddler
134–135	The Penguin
136–139	Poison Ivy
140–141	Two-Face
142–145	Scarecrow
146–147	Killer Croc
148–151	Mr. Freeze
152–153	Bane
154–157	Clayface
158–159	Rogues Gallery

Life doesn't give you seatbelts •
Storyboard art, David Tuber

160–161 **Vehicles**
162–165   The Batmobile
166–169   The Ultimate Batmobile
170–171   The Batwing
172–173   The Scuttler
174–175   Batcave Vehicles
176–179   The Joker's Notorious Lowrider
180–181   Bane's Toxic Truck
182–183   The Catcycle
184–185   The Riddle Racer
186–187   Scarecopter
188–191   Two-Face's Excavator
192–193   The Arctic Roller
194–195   Killer Croc's Tail-Gator
196–197   Harley Quinn's Cannon Truck
           & Egghead's Mech

198–200   Acknowledgments

FOREWORDS

The first LEGO® movie was a seven-year process from the initial idea to the film's release, and making it proved an amazingly fun yet creative challenge. As soon as THE LEGO MOVIE hit theaters, the joy, irreverence, and emotional themes in the film resonated with audiences around the world, and with kids and adults alike. The enthusiasm to see more stories told in the imaginative medium of LEGO toys was palpable.

During this time, LEGO Batman—and Will Arnett's spin on the character—gathered his own fan base larger than any of us could have anticipated. The fresh take on a well-established DC Comics Super Hero was fun for adults who were already familiar with his legacy, and for children who had learned about him through animated interpretations.

We therefore approached the studio and the LEGO Group with the idea of making a standalone LEGO BATMAN MOVIE. We also brought back our key team members to work together again, having had so much fun making the first movie.

When assembling these movies from the beginning, we always start with an emotional question to explore over the course of the story. For this movie, given all the Batman stories we've seen before, we asked ourselves: why is the best night-stalking, crime-fighting vigilante, who has all the best toys and lives in a mansion, so sad and lonely all the time? What if he were confronted with a problem too big to solve on his own, and had to accept other people into his life? We've had a blast exploring a side of Batman's character that audiences haven't seen before. A vulnerable side, underneath the cowl.

Here in the pages of this book is a peek into the great thought, detail, and process that the creative teams across the world undertook over the course of three years to bring THE LEGO BATMAN MOVIE to audiences of all ages. We hope you enjoy both this book and the film as much as we've enjoyed being a part of this Super Hero story alongside Warner Bros., the LEGO Group, and Animal Logic.

Director Chris McKay and
Producers Dan Lin, Phil Lord, and Chris Miller

We are excited to share with you a special behind-the-scenes look at the collaboration and creativity that has gone into the making of THE LEGO® BATMAN MOVIE. As an executive producer on both the THE LEGO BATMAN MOVIE and THE LEGO MOVIE, I have had the amazing opportunity to be part of the collaborative journey between the LEGO Group and Warner Bros. from the very beginning.

For LEGO Batman, that journey began in 2014, when we first started to imagine what his home town of Gotham City might look like if it was completely built out of LEGO pieces. We became even more excited when we started exploring what LEGO Batman might get up to in this unique and never-before-seen version of the iconic DC location. It was only through bringing together the creativity and imagination of the LEGO toy brand with the originality and passion of a truly wonderful group of filmmakers that we could solve the central question, which eventually became the cornerstone of our joint movie: "Can LEGO Batman be happy?"

We hope you enjoy diving deep into the world of THE LEGO BATMAN MOVIE and the animation development process that went into creating it in this book. You will find extensive behind-the-scenes insights and images that show the work that went into the making of the movie. The dedication of both the LEGO and Warner Bros. teams to make sure every detail in the movie lives up to the LEGO motto of "Only the best is good enough," is evident in these pages.

Just as LEGO Batman figured out that working together as a team is actually more fun than working alone, I think I can say unequivocally that we had a blast making this movie together!

Jill Wilfert
Executive Producer and Vice President of
Licensing & Entertainment for the LEGO Group

TIMELINE

The making of THE LEGO® BATMAN MOVIE was a fun ride through the animation production process. Here's a guided tour of the adventure, stopping at some of its creative milestones to give an idea of the whos, hows, and whats involved in the journey—step by step and brick by brick.

1. BATMAN BEGINNINGS

THE LEGO BATMAN MOVIE is the cinematic combination of two well-loved pop culture legacies that have been inspiring the worldwide collective imagination for nearly a century. "The LEGO brand is surprise and invention," says Producer Chris Miller, "and risk-taking and creativity," adds Phil Lord, fellow Producer and long-time partner in crime and filmmaking. The realm of DC characters is that of "Super Heroes, which are our Greek gods, our archetypes, and just a lot of fun," notes Director Chris McKay. When LEGO Batman appeared onscreen in THE LEGO® MOVIE™, the cast of filmmakers realized that he would be a breakout character—one that audiences really wanted to spend more time with, and one that these filmmakers really wanted to explore as well.

2. COLLABORATION AROUND THE WORLD

Development and production of the movie involved collaboration around the world. Concept, character, story, and script were shared between the Warner Bros. Studio in California and Animal Logic in Australia. Animal Logic also handled the physical film production, while the LEGO Group in Denmark generated ideas for character and vehicle modeling and then developed them. These three collaborators communicated freely on ideas, artwork, and LEGO models by way of meetings, video-conferencing, and shared software. They set out to craft an entertaining film that would tell an authentic DC Super Hero story, brought to life with the famous charm and imagination of the LEGO medium. At the very heart of the story was the idea of a deep, complex character realizing there is more to life than he thinks. Director Chris McKay describes developing this idea as "a great sandbox to play in."

Team building • Designers at the LEGO headquarters in Denmark channeled their collective creativity to brainstorm and build new vehicles to appear in the film.

The other side of the world • Generating ideas and reviewing scenes was a continuous process at the Animal Logic animation studios in Sydney, Australia.

3. SCRIPT AND STORYBOARDS

Scripting and storyboarding for the movie ran side by side. The writers and story artists inspired each other as they strove to express humor, emotion, and action through visuals and dialogue. "Like every animated movie, the story went through dozens of iterations between different drafts of the script and different storyboard versions—but something we locked in on almost from the start was: 'Can Batman be happy?'" recalls writer Seth Grahame-Smith. This theme made the movie more than an action-packed, funny adventure. It made it a roller coaster of emotions with positive messages, "... exactly what we look for from a LEGO point of view," says LEGO Vice President of Design Matthew Ashton. Story artists portray suggested dialogue and action in storyboards—a succession of panels that tell a story in a similar way to a comic book (see p.8). Storyboards may be roughly sketched or fully illustrated and colored. They often serve as the first shot-by-shot visual translation of the script.

```
                    RIDDLER
          Riddle me this!  What rhymes with
          Teddy...

                    JOKER
               (on walkie)
          Can you just say yes or no?

Beat.

                    RIDDLER
          Yes.

INT. COCKPIT

                    JOKER
          Perfect!  I sure hope Gotham City
          is wearing a giant diaper, because
          they're about to get a load of me!

EXT. GOTHAM ENERGY FACILITY - GUARD BOOTH

A FIGURE approaches SECURITY GUARD STEVE in a pizza delivery
truck.

                    PIZZA DELIVERY SONG
          I scream, you scream, we all scream
          for pizza!

                    FIGURE (SCARECROW)
          Pizza delivery.

                    SECURITY GUARD SANDY
          All right!  I love pizza!

                    FIGURE (SCARECROW)
          Great!  The toppings are sausage,
          anchovies,and fear gas!

SCARECROW releases his fear gas, causing Security Guard Sally
to hallucinate SCARY PIZZA HALLUCINATIONS.

                    SECURITY GUARD SANDY
          Uhhhh.....

                    SCARY PIZZA HALLUCINATION
          Don't touch the alarm!

In follows TRUCKS driven by VARIOUS VILLAINS.
```

Word play • A script provides structure and dialogue for the movie. This script developed in tandem with storyboarding.

4. ANIMATIC

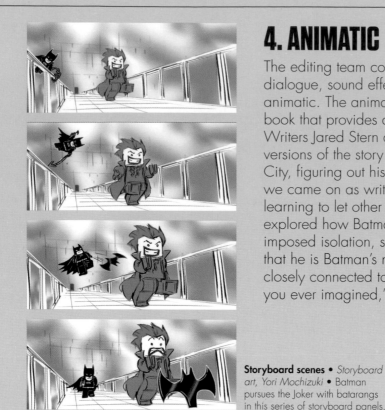

The editing team combined storyboard images with temporary dialogue, sound effects, and music to create a story reel, or animatic. The animatic is essentially a moving, speaking comic book that provides a rough cut of how the sequence will play. Writers Jared Stern and John Whittington recall that earlier versions of the story featured Batman in a crime-free Gotham City, figuring out his place in this new world, but "by the time we came on as writers, the focus was more about Batman learning to let other people into his life." The story team explored how Batman might handle intrusions upon his self-imposed isolation, such as the Joker asking for acknowledgment that he is Batman's nemesis. "Batman learns that you need to be closely connected to others to be your best self, stronger than you ever imagined," explains Story Supervisor Trisha Gum.

Storyboard scenes • *Storyboard art, Yori Mochizuki* • Batman pursues the Joker with batarangs in this series of storyboard panels.

5. PRODUCTION DESIGN

The production design team began establishing the overall "look" for the film. Grant Freckelton at Animal Logic encouraged his artistic team to create a fresh new perspective for the movie while keeping to the traditions of both DC Comics and LEGO toys. Thousands of concepts were drafted and vetted among all three creative collaborators. Initial designs were done by both Animal Logic and the LEGO team, with the requirements of each character, vehicle, or location dictating which company played the leading role. Throughout the process, the Warner Bros. team ensured that a DC vibe was maintained. Geometry and color were important considerations—designers worked with pieces and palettes that existed or could be newly created in the LEGO realm. To create a really authentic LEGO look, all characters and vehicles seen in the movie went through a very similar process to that used when creating the real LEGO toys.

> "We didn't make any quick decisions in this process: every aspect of every vehicle and character was thought through and debated."
>
> **Michael Fuller, LEGO Senior Design Manager**

First impressions • *Concept art, Tim Pyman and Paul Constantin Turcanu* • Thousands of environment, character, and vehicle concepts were crafted by Animal Logic and the LEGO Group in the visual development of production design.

6. ART DIRECTION

The art direction team focused their attention on capturing the mood and color for key moments in the film. Grayscale images were used to convey lighting situations, and vibrant colorscript images were used to paint full-color scenes. The team wanted the film to look dark and moody, yet at the same time full of light and color. Solving that contradiction was quite a challenge, but as Production Designer Grant Freckelton remarks, "challenges are what makes the process fun and the final result unique." All color choices were guided by an existing LEGO palette of 57 colors. "This might seem like a small amount to work with, but we really came to embrace it," says Art Director Vivienne To. The art direction team also took into account how lighting and effects might change the colors onscreen.

Spot of color • *Colorscripts on screen; colorscript images* • Colorscript paintings inform color and lighting choices for key moments in the film.

7. VOICE TALENT

Once the animatic was finalized, the dialogue for the final film was recorded. Casting a character's voice is a fun but challenging task, since its pacing and emotional texture has a big effect on the animation performance. "Will Arnett plays Batman as a really arrogant guy, but there's a vulnerability deep underneath that shines through his voice all of the time," says Producer Chris Miller. Robin was voiced by Michael Cera "with sweetness and honesty, like a super-positive kid who really just wants a hug," notes Director Chris McKay. Then there is the villain, the Joker, who is voiced by Zach Galifianakis. Producer Phil Lord describes Zach as the kind of comedian who you're a little bit scared of—afraid of what he might say. "We really like that feeling of comedic danger that's in his performance," explains Lord. While voice talent artists worked to a script, they were welcome to adlib a little, bringing an extra sparkle to their minifigure personas.

From microphone to minifigure • Actors recorded dialogue for which animators crafted expressions and actions, bringing minifigures to life in the film.

Delving into DC history • Filmmakers reached into the comic chronicles of Batman for artistic and story inspiration.

8. RESEARCH AND DEVELOPMENT

Research and development were important throughout the process of creating THE LEGO BATMAN MOVIE. Filmmakers searched the DC archive to find characters for the Rogues Gallery and planted a wealth of bonus details from DC lore within the film to delight DC aficionados. Artists also had to familiarize themselves with the library of LEGO pieces (including new ones made specifically for the film), and the production design team visited the LEGOLAND® Park to research LEGO environments in epic scale. On the software side, translating huge "LEGOscapes" into animation models and creating brick motion blur were just a couple of the challenges. Ambitious lighting and shading needs led to the creation of new systems at Animal Logic, such as the shading system Ash and the image-rendering program Glimpse. These made it possible to apply variable textures to LEGO bricks and characters with high efficiency—important when processing millions upon millions of detailed bricks.

A study in bricks • Artists studied physical LEGO bricks in great detail to understand and reinterpret them for the CG realm. Colorists became well-versed in the LEGO palette in order to create authentic LEGO creations in a virtual world.

9. MODELING

This was the phase that really got into the joy of LEGO toys: building characters, props, and environments using the 3,286 (at the last count) pieces across 45 different element types. Model concepts on this movie began with either the Animal Logic or LEGO design teams. Then the models went through rigorous notes sessions and versions involving all three creative collaborators before anything was fully built in the CG world. "Once a rough build is approved with simple geometry, we replace the simple geometry with brick-built models in the building program LEGO Digital Designer (LDD). We then do a set-dressing pass, adding bits of detail to give the models a finished, lived-in look," explains Modeling Supervisor Bradley Sick.

Constructing structures • *Animation development and final renders* • More than 75 full movie sets were modeled for THE LEGO BATMAN MOVIE.

10. RIGGING

Next, models that would move in the film were given rigging controls, which allowed them to be poseable but not too flexible, as they needed to move like plastic bricks rather than real-life humans or vehicles. It was a balancing act to create "an endearing character, one that cannot pose unrealistically but at the same time allows enough creative freedom," explains Rigging Lead Josh Murtack. For example, a minifigure's claw-shaped hand can flex outward slightly when something is pushed into it, but it will never exhibit the squash and stretch of a cartoon character.

Motion control • *Animation screenshot* • The film's characters' movements stayed fairly true to those of real minifigures.

11. LOOK DEVELOPMENT

Models and characters were then put through the look development process to be given surfaces and textures, with an aim to making them appear as photo-real as possible. "We try to capture and represent what we see on a LEGO brick when looking through a magnifying glass," notes Look Development Supervisor J.P. Le Blanc. "Some texturing is applied by default. It is then manipulated by an artist who adds in detailing that mimics a LEGO brick's manufacture, mold markings, and real-world scuffs and fingerprints."

Minifigure in the making • *Animation development* • Step-by-step modeling images show Poison Ivy's development from blank minifigure to fully clad Rogue.

> "A typical LEGO minifigure might have 10 pieces, but some of the vehicles for this film had well over 2,000. No animation software on the market can handle that many individual objects, so we developed new tools to be able to manage these."

Josh Murtack, Rigging Lead

Shot development • *Scene layout screenshot* • Multiple camera angles are developed during the layout phase.

12. LAYOUT

The layout phase took the animatic stage to the next level and kicked off the production pipeline for animation. It involved replacing storyboard images with actual models and suggested camera angles with final camera movements. "Layout" is also where the sense of scale is established, and the goal for this film was to create an epic feel. The team started by setting the size of vehicles a bit larger than the typical LEGO vehicle, moving them up from the standard six studs wide to eight. "Although two extra studs doesn't feel like a lot, it allows for more detail and for two minifigures to sit side by side inside," notes Production Designer Grant Freckelton. From there, proportionate neighborhoods were placed in each shot, character stand-ins were positioned, and the shot was passed along for animation.

13. ANIMATION

Working in the LEGO medium is a fun challenge for animators, as there are inherent limitations to moving rigid plastic characters. Animation Supervisor Rob Coleman notes that while the team stayed true to the range of motion of a minifigure, movement was portrayed by the characters in a brilliant way: "Instead of squishing the LEGO pieces, we spread them apart momentarily and then click them back together, so at film speed the audience feels the squash and stretch rather than seeing it." Animators also used LEGO pieces that had been converted into "particles." This meant they could isolate individual pieces in a scene and do specialized things with them. Perhaps most notably, the animation team developed extensive facial expressions for each minifigure to make characters more emotive.

Face off • *Animation screenshots* • Animators could pick the perfect facial expressions for a scene to help minifigures better connect with the audience.

Go low • *Scene layout screenshot* • Clever camera angles and techniques help the audience to get a sense of the epic scale of the LEGO film sets.

14. VIRTUAL CINEMATOGRAPHY

Cinematography is the art of blending camera and lighting work to create an immersive experience for the audience. "We wanted everything to feel small, yet epic and cinematic," explains Head of Layout Behzad Mansoori-Dara. To achieve this, the team limited the number of close-up shots to remind the audience of how tiny the minifigure characters really are. Setting the camera angles at a shallow depth of field further enhanced the feel of miniature photography, by bringing the minifigure characters into focus and separating them from the background. "The look of our CG images evokes the memory of when you were a kid playing with LEGO sets on the floor of your room," says Stereoscopic Supervisor Fabian Müller.

15. EFFECTS

In order to remain authentic to the LEGO medium but give the film a truly cinematic feel, the film's effects team combined brick-based effects for destruction, fire, and explosions with photo-real effects for smoke and water. The team studied special effects used in previous Batman films and various stop-motion videos. They even filmed their own reference for what LEGO models look like in smoky and wet environments. In the film's opening sequence, a cargo plane emerges through cloud cover. The team captured the fine details of dry ice swirling, and added interaction from the body of the LEGO cargo plane and its propellers, "all within a shot that was over a thousand frames long," recalls Effects Supervisor Miles Green. This single shot required such complex work by Effects Artist Jayandera Danappal that work on it took almost three months to complete.

Very special effects • *Effects simulations screenshots* • Animal Logic created many brick-based effects for the film, including various types of explosions.

16. LIGHTING

The LEGO world is all about color, while the world of DC Comics movies is traditionally about theatrical lighting. Bringing these two characteristics into alignment was a real artistic challenge. "We can completely alter the mood of a scene by changing the color of the light," notes Production Designer Grant Freckelton. With the use of Maya and Ash software, the lighting team created the look that "characters were embedded in a vibrantly colorful world without getting lost in the mosaic of color," explains Lighting Supervisor Craig Welsh. Characters and other objects of interest in a shot were at least partly illuminated by a neutral light source, which accentuated the real-world LEGO colors. Lighting also helped create recognizable character silhouettes, enabling the audience to immediately identify characters that have the same minifigure shape as each other.

Light my fire • *Animation development* • The film's lighting team gradually built up a sense of the natural warmth of firelight in this series of images.

17. COMPOSITING AND RENDERING

Compositing and rendering efforts pull together all of the previous work on shots to create the images that appear on the big screen. In a LEGO built world, CG renders tend to have a clean and clinical look, so the film's compositing team sought to "beat them up enough to make them look like they were shot with real-life lenses in our flawed physical reality," notes Compositing Supervisor Alex Fry. This effect was accomplished in Glimpse rendering software, by adding the optical imperfections that make real objects look the way they do when photographed, such as lens flare and light diffusion.

Editing in progress • Editing was carried out in Animal Logic's open-plan offices throughout the film's development process.

18. EDITING

The editing process took place throughout the entire production of the film, starting with the assembly of storyboard animatics and continuing as each stage of animation work was completed. The editorial team established timing and pacing, for playing out moments of drama or comedy. "A lot of the comedy moments come from the dramatic situations the characters are placed in. I wouldn't say strict rules apply to editing comedy versus drama, but I would say that editing comedy is more difficult!" says Editor David Burrows. The use of temporary music and effects during the editing process further fed into the emotion of the film, and was key to engaging the audience on a deeper level.

19. MUSIC AND SOUND PRODUCTION

After the film's dialogue was recorded and the editorial team had established pacing and timing in sequences, final music and sound effects were added to the film. "In most cases, these sound elements carry the message of the story that the filmmakers want to tell," says Sound Designer Wayne Pashley. One of the fun things about working in a LEGO world is the opportunity for really imaginative sound effects to come into play. Instead of gunshots, firearms in the film made the vocal sound of "pew, pew, pew, pew, pew, pew." As for the film's musical score, Lorne Balfe crafted a soundtrack that "strikes the perfect balance between a super exciting Batman action movie and a heartwearming movie that reveals a side to Batman never seen before," notes Editor David Burrows. The use of rock and pop songs throughout the film also added to the pace and emotion of scenes, as well as reflecting Batman's mindset at any given moment.

Musical notes • Sound Designer Wayne Pashley adds sound to the movie to musicalize the humor, emotion, and action.

> **"**When you're dealing with comedy, a sound can easily make or break the moment.**"**
>
> **Wayne Pashley, Sound Designer**

Glasses on • Filmmakers at Animal Logic analyzed THE LEGO BATMAN MOVIE in a stereoscopic review, part of the constant evaluation process at the animation studio.

20. FINAL MIX

Picture and sound fully came together at the final mix stage, when each and every element was brought into proper alignment for the big screen. On the visual side, colors were adjusted shot by shot to convey the desired optical effect. The stereoscopic (or 3-D) experience was studied to make sure that production choices allowed an enjoyable (and not jarring) effect for the audience. This was especially true in action sequences where fast motion may have been hard to track or caused a sense of motion sickness for viewers. On the sound side, dialogue, effects, and music were tweaked to make sure each sound was presented at its optimum volume, whether it was a quiet sniffle, a roaring engine, or a booming rock song.

21. REAL-WORLD LEGO® SETS

From the earliest idea stages of the film, LEGO designers were on the lookout for assets that would make the coolest LEGO toy sets, so that imaginative play could continue off-screen as well. "We are fully involved with model development from day one so that we can insure that every one is built in a manner that can be translated into reality," explains LEGO Senior Design Manager Michael Fuller. The design process for characters and vehicles in the film was the same as that for regular toy development, except those builds would also be scrutinized in high definition, big-screen detail. "It's incredibly important that every detail is perfect, and that the models can perform in the way they need to to tell the story," adds LEGO Vice President of Design Matthew Ashton. From a toy perspective, the LEGO Group considered how a child would play with the real model, so rigorous quality checks and safety testing also came into play. The LEGO Group has a long history with DC, but this project took that relationship to a new level. Many existing DC minifigures were reimagined and made over, with some receiving new elements—hairstyles, belts, and other accessories—creating a fresh new identity for such historic characters.

Ready for playtime • The LEGO design team considered a multitude of costume designs for the movie's various Rogues during the film's production process.

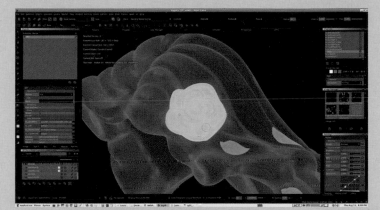

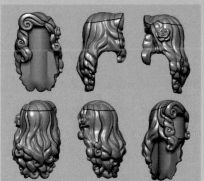

Down to the details • *Animation screenshot; animation development* • LEGO designers informed the filmmakers of the tiniest production details on the real minifigures they produced, so filmmakers could incorporate those same details in their animations.

> "Everyone loves Batman. Everyone loves LEGO toys. There's a lot of responsibility in making sure we follow through and produce something great by merging these two worlds successfully."
>
> **Michael Fuller, LEGO Senior Design Manager**

22. EPILOGUE

"Growing up, I loved the imaginative stuff we'd do with toys inspired by movies, with action figures and a bucket of LEGO bricks. You'd build stuff and play with various toys like a mash-up, and it didn't seem weird or like worlds were colliding," recalls Director Chris McKay, who now enjoys the process in reverse, bringing toys to the movie realm. Just as LEGO Batman learns that teamwork is a good thing, the creative collaborators that came together to make this film certainly followed that storyline themselves. Their collaboration shows that LEGO toys are the perfect medium to inspire and innovate imaginative play, and that the world of Batman is the ideal setting to explore that creative effort.

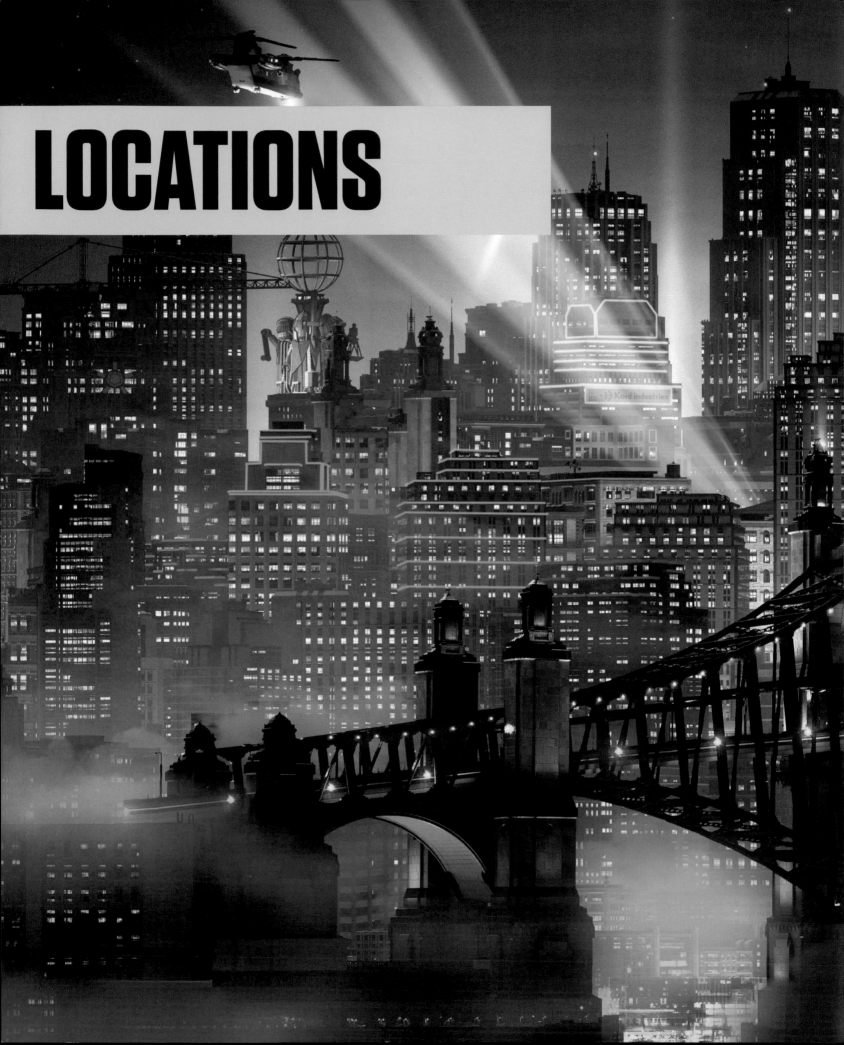

LOCATIONS

WAYNE MANOR

Wayne Manor is the grandest of grand mansions, whether it exists in comic books or the LEGO® world. In creating a fitting residence for billionaire Bruce Wayne, the art team were inspired by the mansions of the American Gilded Age. These stately designs reflect Bruce's deep pockets, but also a sense of isolation that is just right for the brooding hero.

Home solid home • *Concept art, Grant Freckelton* • These three architectural concepts of Wayne Manor cover different design styles, from dark art deco towers to a mountainous Jacobean castle and a flatland Neo-Gothic country estate.

Far and away • *Concept art, Vivienne To* • These explorations take Wayne Manor off into distant landscapes, a concept that resonates with the isolated life Bruce chooses to lead.

Gated grandeur • *Concept art, Adam Duncan* • Nothing says "Welcome" better than entry via limousine through a sculptural steel gateway. Entrants then pass over a chasm along an arch bridge, traverse a winding hillside, and climb up to a castle on a precipice.

Closer to construction • *Final render* • This colorful "lit shot" shows off the LEGO brick-built Wayne Manor, with its Gotham City backdrop in place.

Island of solitude • *Final art* •
This painting of the finalized Wayne
Manor portrays a solitary castle atop
a tall mountain surrounded by water.

"The attention to detail in the set design and set dressing is breathtaking."

Laurence Andrews, Layout Lead

INSIDE WAYNE MANOR

More than 75 sets were created for the movie, from large cityscapes to small, intimate interiors, such as Bruce Wayne's screening room. No detail was missed when designing the inside of Wayne Manor. The Dining Hall is lined with paintings depicting famous moments in history, as well as vacation images of Bruce, Martha, and Thomas Wayne. The tables are even arranged to form a simplified "W" shape.

Gallery of good times • *Graphic art, Nadia Attlee •* Portraits and snapshots of the Wayne family stare out at Bruce, reminding him of a life of happiness long since departed from Wayne Manor.

Dinner, party of one • *Concept art, Matt Hatton •* Bruce Wayne has the best and loneliest seat in Wayne Manor's Dining Hall, but at least there is nothing to distract him from appreciating the room in all its vaulted, gilded, ornamental glory. The large, empty space makes the solitary minifigure appear all the more miniaturized.

Fabulous fun ... for one • *Concept art, Thomas Zenteno and Adam Duncan* • Wayne Manor has a gourmet kitchen (with microwave for Lobster Thermidor for one), a gorgeous pool, a private theater, and even a fashion show runway ... but none of these amazing spaces fill the empty space around Bruce's heart. In fact, their dramatic lighting and huge scale only make him feel smaller and lonelier.

Frothing the frown • *Concept art (top), Thomas Zenteno; final render (bottom)* •
Wayne Manor's master bathroom is adorned with nautical niceties. Surely brushing his
teeth with water spouted into the sink by a golden fish has to make Batman smile?

"The mask hardly ever comes off,
physically and figuratively. It's what makes
Bruce feel safe and unexposed."

Chris McKay, Director

Pastime pictures • *Graphic art, Nadia Attlee* • The bathroom walls are filled with reminders of all the fun things Batman does … by himself. He looks at them when he has nothing but idle time to think in the bathroom … by himself.

JOKERIZED WAYNE MANOR

When Batman is out of the way, the Joker invades Wayne Manor and makes a joke out of the place—quite literally. In the Joker's scheme for the Manor, the grand estate is transformed into a theme park gone mad.

JOKER'S "THEME PARK"—
RIDES AND ATTRACTIONS
INCLUDE PRANKS AND
DIRTY TRICKS . . .

. . . LIKE A ROLLER COASTER TRACK
THAT ENDS MID-AIR, AND CARS THAT LAND
ON A TRAMPOLINE THAT EITHER DOES
OR DOESN'T BOUNCE THEM BACK
INTO THE RIDE DEPENDING ON CHANCE . . .

. . . ANOTHER "SUCKER" RIDE THAT
RANDOMLY DUMPS RECLAIMED
WATER ON GUESTS . . .

Punchline lineworks • *Concept art, Chris Reccardi* • The jokes keep rolling and rolling. These concept pieces, sketched and colored over an original Wayne Manor image, suggest how the Joker's flying "J" banners, tricks, and pranks might overrun the once-respectable mansion.

Troubling tracks • *Concept art, Matt Hatton* • Sketch artwork expands the fairground
style into a full-blown theme park—a further exploration of the Joker's scheme.

Joker Manor • *Final render* • Smart and sedate Wayne
Manor (just visible) has undergone a Jokerized remodel
in this final model render.

THE BATCAVE

The "wow factor" was undoubtedly a priority in designing the Batcave. The movie's production team sought to create a space that was off the charts in terms of scale and technology—and to have a little fun with parody when it came to their super subject matter. Depth, width, and breadth certainly seem infinite upon first impression. In fact, if it was actually built in LEGO bricks the entire Batcave would be 91.2 meters (299.2 feet) long—mammoth compared to its tiny owner. The Batcave is also full of contradictions, with cutting edge technology surrounded by natural rock.

"Look closely in the Batcave and you can see vehicles that span the history of Batman and various trophies and 'easter eggs.'"

Amber Naismith, Producer

Underground wonder-ground • *Concept art, Grant Freckelton and Adam Duncan* • The Batcave's enormity become clear in this piece. Robotic platforms and devices parody the over-engineered technology in other Super Hero movies, but also show Batman's reliance on machines rather than humans.

Make it bigger • *Concept art, Kelly Baigent and Charles Santaso* • Influenced by large-scale industrial spaces such as airport hangars, oil refineries, and car factories, the design team used the word "ludicrous" to describe the intended size of the Batcave.

What's the angle? • *Concept art, Adam Duncan* • The grand scale and immense amount of detail in the Batcave present a cinematographic challenge: how to place the camera in a way that shows off this impressive set while still focusing the viewer on the characters and their action within it.

Monitor mayhem • *Concept art, Adam Duncan* • Views of the Batcomputer overwhelm the eye with a vast array of cables, platforms, control panels, and display screens, giving a highly technical but slightly chaotic feel to the space.

BATCAVE TECHNOLOGY

Art direction portrays the heart of the Batcave as a complicated, overwhelming, and somewhat over-engineered space. It's a control center designed to make Batman a better Super Hero, but it also enables him to rely more on hardware than humankind. According to the production design team, this space is awesome in one sense, but sad in another—ultimately making it "sadsome"!

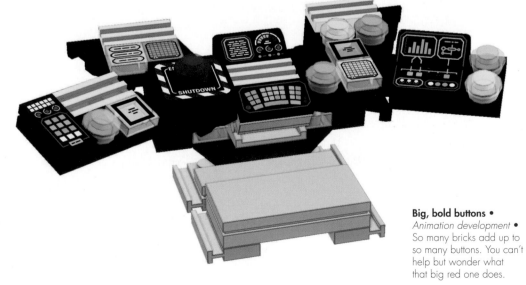

Big, bold buttons • *Animation development* • So many bricks add up to so many buttons. You can't help but wonder what that big red one does.

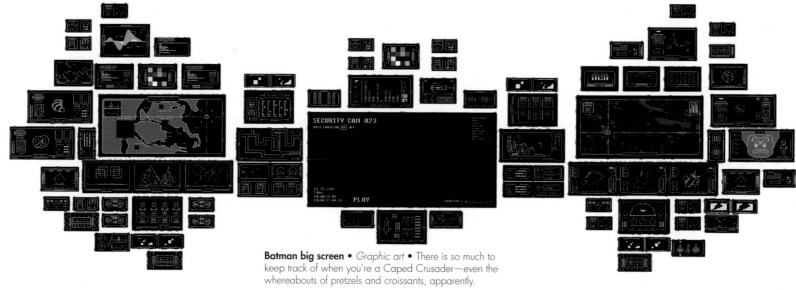

Batman big screen • *Graphic art* • There is so much to keep track of when you're a Caped Crusader—even the whereabouts of pretzels and croissants, apparently.

"To pull off shots in this set, we had to dip into our entire bag of tricks … but once lit, these shots became some of the most striking and iconic in the film."

Jeff Renton, Layout and Assembly Supervisor

Select by task or attitude • *Concept art, Thomas Zenteno* • What mood or mission will determine today's Batsuit choice? Countless detailed options were developed for the contents of Batman's wardrobe, even though they will only be glimpsed for a moment in the movie.

BATCAVE GARAGE

The production design team were inspired by comics and real-world car storage systems in their efforts to make the Batcave vehicle housing an incredible and effective set. The garage contains myriad Batmobiles, many of which are previously released official LEGO Bat-vehicles. They're all displayed on a rotisserie-style contraption, which earned the set the nickname of the "Spice Rack" from the crew during development. The finished model's gears, platforms, ramps, and overall engineering are mind-blowing—just as everything in the Batcave should be.

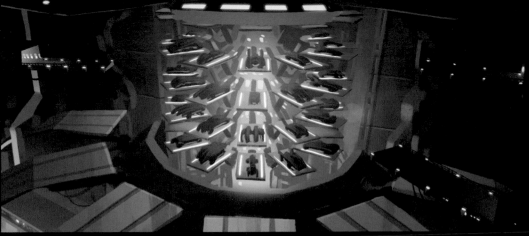

Heavy-duty hydraulics • *Concept art (left and top), Matt Hatton and Adam Duncan; animation development (middle); final render (bottom)* • This progression shows the garage and the evolution of the animation: 1. A detailed line drawing highlights the geometric elements; 2. Painted concept art shows the placement within the Batcave; 3. The development of the LEGO build of the model clearly shows the mechanical complexity; 4. A final render includes full surfacing, environmental effects, and lighting. This section of the Batcave alone shows how impressive the set's 15,000 lights look when illuminated.

BATCAVE HANGAR

In the air, Batman is in his element. What you see in the hangar area of the Batcave demonstrates just how over-the-top his collection of vehicles is. The production design team visually answer the question of "What would a Batcave be like if someone had literally billions and billions and billions of dollars at their disposal and also an ego to match that amount of money?"

Every kind of transport • *Concept art, Adam Duncan and Matt Hatton* • The Batcave has transportation to cover the chasing of criminals high and low, and then some. While some of the flying Bat-vehicles shown here have appeared in previous Batman stories, others were brand new. The production design team had fun expanding his collection, utilizing the imaginative options of the LEGO medium.

GOTHAM CITY

Gotham City is as iconic as Batman himself. A sprawling metropolitan community, it has long been likened to New York City, but in this movie it's first and foremost part of the LEGO world. Inspiration for this version of Gotham City was drawn partly from past representations found in comics, television, and film, and partly from real-world vintage sources, including city street photography from the 1970s. It's an impressively massive place, with a gritty, retro feel.

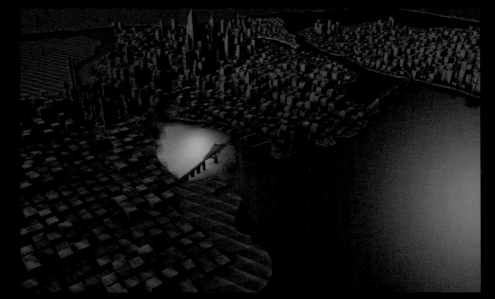

Urban sprawl • *Animation development, Laurence Andrews* • To explore scale and silhouette, the modeling team built rough models of Gotham City. Beyond the specialized Gotham Circle and skyscrapers, approximately 100 generic buildings were built, with variable numbers of floors and rooftops that could make thousands of configurations. These were then placed in the established boundaries of Gotham City, grouped to create distinct neighborhoods with buildings of a certain size, height, and style.

PORT OF GOTHAM

"We knew early on that we wanted to give Gotham City a timeless quality."

Grant Freckelton, Production Designer

The city comes alive • *Concept art, Adam Duncan and Grant Freckelton* • Gotham City is more like a character than just a location in DC lore. This progression of shots from line drawing to tonal to color key shows the city has presence, depth, and vibrancy in the LEGO world, too.

Brick-built buildings • *Animation development* • This environment render of Gotham
Circle shows how an initial sketch (top) is translated into a working animation.

A spin around the Circle • *Concept art, Adam Duncan* • A sketched panoramic view of Gotham Circle shows the intense architectural detail involved in planning the space.

A dark night in Gotham City • *Concept art, Adam Duncan* • This concept art explores how Gotham City might look after an influx of villains from the Phantom Zone corrupts the city.

CITY SCENES

A huge set, Gotham City is made from the same basic building blocks, yet has a realistic feel because of thoughtful use of detail. Neighborhoods are given character through the use of pieces of street dressing, such as air-conditioners, fire escapes, street lights, and billboards. The team took great care to ensure that Gotham City appears run down, just as it does in classic depictions, by giving the structures a neglected and weathered look. Using shading programs to create dirt, grunge, chipping, and decay allowed the team to provide believable levels of grime. Each billboard in Gotham Circle was carefully hand treated so the jokes remained legible through the wear and tear.

Have a seat • *Final render* • Shoddy Street depicts more of the run-down nature of the city. It's decorated with overflowing trash cans, burned-out cars, and abandoned furniture—including a worn-out version of Emmet's double-decker couch from THE LEGO® MOVIE™ (on the sidewalk to the right of the burning vehicle). This scene makes particular use of the Look Development team's shading programs, which add grunge to the corners and crevices of LEGO brick assemblies.

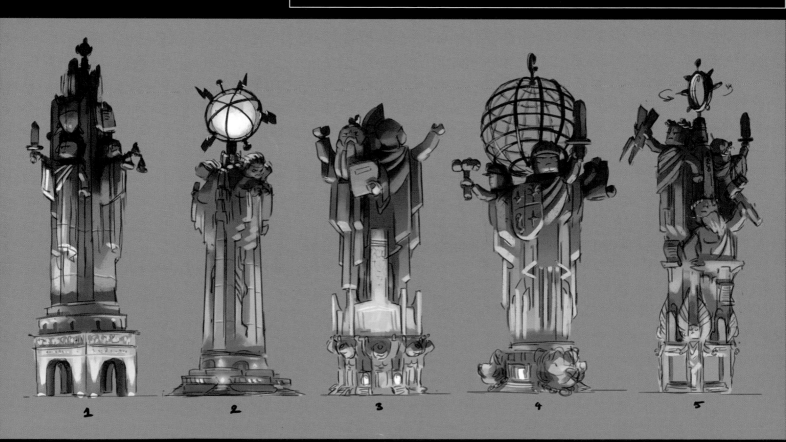

1   2   3   4   5

Civic pride • *Concept art, Adam Duncan* • Plans for a grandiose public monument amongst the grit and grime of the streets help convey a sense of a city with a proud history that has buckled under years of crime and corruption.

City center • *Concept art, Grant Freckelton and Adam Duncan* • At the heart of the city is Gotham Circle, a mix of 1970s Times Square and Piccadilly Circus. It has a bustling abundance of traffic and billboards, and, at its center, a truly monumental statue—a nostalgic parody to the giant statues seen in earlier Batman films.

Licensed vehicles • LEGO *model development, Adam Grabowski* • The width of cars had to be decided early on, as this informed the width of roads and the scale of the whole city. Some of these detailed, eight-stud-wide cars include plates with designers' initials.

Sprayed-on sets • *Graphic art, Nadia Attlee* • Graffiti on the Gotham City subway cars looks like it has been carried out by some roguish villains, and one Master Builder with a cameo. A tag appears to be from THE LEGO MOVIE's Wyldstyle—Batman's ex-girlfriend!

City dwellers • *Concept art, Nadia Attlee* • Gotham City's citizens are diverse in their ethnic backgrounds and ages, as well as in their fashion sensibilities. Even though these characters are meant for background population only, there isn't a hairstyle, outfit, or accessory that isn't carefully considered. Initially, the art team considered a retro look for the civilians, mirroring the 70s vibe of Gotham City itself. This direction was later parked and a more current look was applied to the characters.

GOTHAM CABLE NEWS 6PM

GCN

WHEN NEWS BREAKS, WE PUT THE PIECES TOGETHER

Is it a bird? Is it a plane?
Yep, it's a plane.

Daily non stop flights to Metropolis with *Ferris* **AIR**

BIG BELLY BURGER
HOME OF THE CLOGGER
More burger for your belly...

Plastique PARFUM

Plastique PARFUM

MUSK OF THE PHANTASM

JAZZ CLUB
OPEN 9:00 PM TIL LATE

VOTE FOR **HARVEY DENT**
For a better Gotham City

Janus COSMETICS

Crustacean Station
FAMILY SEAFOOD RESTAURANT

GOTHAM ART GALLERY
PORTRAIT COLLECTION
Winter Season Exhibition

On *Furst Avenue* THE MUSICAL

SONGS! THE MUSICAL

GOT HAM?
MAKE SURE IT'S LAZLO'S!
LAZLO'S FINE MEATS

BLACK CANARY
The new album

Minifigure media • *Graphic art, Nadia Attlee and Noemie Cauvin* • *Signage was influenced by photos of New York and Chicago from the 1930s through to the 1980s. Recreating these scenes required many billboard designs, which borrow from DC history and LEGO vocabulary and include references to the crew.*

WAYNE INFLUENCE

Bruce Wayne's sizable contributions to Gotham City were explored early on in the development process with the creation of buildings owned by, or heavily supported by, Wayne Enterprises. And, since Bruce Wayne has buildings of interest dotted around the city, the team also needed to develop a suitably grand way for the man-about-town to get around town.

Sponsorship deals • *Concept art, Adam Duncan* • Wayne Enterprises is involved in all aspects of city life, including providing books for local residents. Citizens can't forget their benefactors when the Wayne logo sits this large on top of the library building.

Ssshhhh ... • *Concept art, Matt Hatton* • Early sketch work shows a grand, well-stocked library, no doubt thanks to generations of Wayne family generosity. An early character exploration suggested that Barbara Gordon once worked as a librarian here.

Ostentatious owner • *Concept art, Adam Duncan* • Classic, modern, and lowrider influences were explored in trying to determine how billionaire Bruce Wayne travels around Gotham City.

Wayne Enterprises • *Concept art, Thomas Zenteno and Matt Hatton* • The architecture of the Wayne Enterprises office lobby once again hints at its eponymous owner, with the art deco styling creating "W" shapes.

GCPD BUILDING

The headquarters for the Gotham City Police Department is the city's proudest landmark—a monument to hope and strength in the never-ending fight against crime. This ambitious LEGO brickwork structure has clear influences of American architect Hugh Ferriss in its tall, lean shape. A minifigure-style goddess of Justice adds a touch of vintage sculpture.

Victory by land, sea, or air • *Concept art, Tim Pyman* • Concept art for GCPD shows an impressive building and diverse vehicles for catching criminals in Gotham City.

Ray of light • *Concept art, Adam Duncan* • Visual development portrays the GCPD building as a shining beacon of hope in the otherwise dark and moody Gotham City.

Police presence • *Animation development* • This image shows the final set in all its brick-built detail, nestled in Gotham City and surrounded by the police parking lot.

Big office for the big guy • *Concept art, Vivienne To* • The art team's initial vision of how Commissioner Jim Gordon's office would look is shown in this concept art. Impressively decorated with numerous trophies and framed photographs, the office had to befit a well-known figure with long service in the Gotham City Police Department.

Police personnel • *Concept art, Vivienne To* • The lineup of Gotham City police officers and detectives is a mixed bag of minifigure men and women. Age, gender, and ethnic background reflect a diverse police force. The art team originally explored a 1970s style of dress. It was later replaced by a modern look, with uniforms designed to cover all of the department's needs.

Badge of honor • *Graphic art* • A police badge must command respect and be instantly recognizable. Creating a simple GCPD badge was an important duty of the graphic designers.

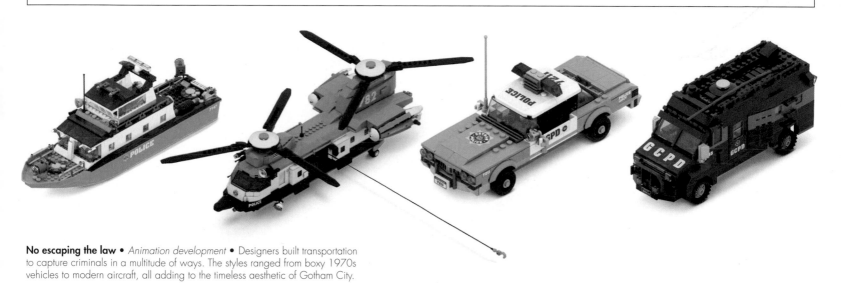

No escaping the law • *Animation development* • Designers built transportation to capture criminals in a multitude of ways. The styles ranged from boxy 1970s vehicles to modern aircraft, all adding to the timeless aesthetic of Gotham City.

Standing proud • *Animation development* • The final Gotham City Police Department design stands out from the buildings around it, thanks to its distinctive shape and the large statue that adorns it. The rounded walls below the GCPD building, curved bridge arches, and varied shapes of the surrounding skyscrapers show the many intricate designs the modeling team can create with LEGO bricks.

CITY HALL

Gotham's City Hall stands tall in all its art deco glory. While interiors were designed for use in earlier versions of the film, the final story utilizes only the exterior of this magnificent brick build. The imposing setting is the location for the glittering Winter Gala, at which the retiring Police Commissioner Gordon hands over his post to his successor.

"We liked the absurdity of people ice-skating in tuxedos and gowns and listening to speeches in the freezing cold. It was as if Gotham's elite will brave any weather to be 'seen.'"

Grant Freckelton, Production Designer

Location, location, location • *Concept art, Adam Duncan •* City Hall is front and center in this geographical mapping of Gotham City.

Fabulous and frozen • *Concept art, Adam Duncan •* The Gala event in this festively colored concept art evokes the charm of New York during the holidays. Ice sculptures depict polar bear angels and Gotham City's elite skate on a glistening ice rink. The scene is packed with detail, including bright lights, limousines, and catering tents.

A tale of three city halls • *Concept art, Adam Duncan* • Variations on Gotham City Hall exhibit influences from buildings such as Los Angeles City Hall, Buffalo City Hall in New York, and Union Terminal in Cincinnati, Ohio.

Gotham City glitz • *Concept art, Fiona Darwin and Nadia Attlee* • Evening gowns start with the same trapezoidal base, yet become a range of fabulously diverse fashions thanks to the LEGO graphic-designer seamstresses. The orphans are dressed in their finest too, hoping to find a wealthy set of parents.

ENERGY FACILITY

The Gotham City Energy Facility is a huge set, built with great detail because of the intense action that takes place around and within the plant. A combination of beautiful architecture and functional industrial design, the LEGO version reflects influences from real-world examples of energy facilities, such as the decommissioned coal-fired power station at Battersea in London.

"Our opening sequence is normally someone else's third act, a big heist with a takeover of the city.**"**

Chris McKay, Director

Then and now • *Concept art (top), Adam Duncan; final render (bottom)* • Between early concept and final render, the guard gate at the Energy Facility took a turn toward realism with surfacing and lighting techniques.

Power over power • *Storyboard art (left), Yori Mochizuki; final render (below)* • Designers looked at outdated control rooms to give a retro feel to the Facility. These images show an early storyboard sketch and its translation into a final film image, complete with new camera angle, set dressing, and lighting to highlight the technical complexity of the plant.

Unsung heroes • *Final render* • Meet foremen David and Dave, upstanding employees of the Energy Facility who are just there to do their jobs and don't want any funny business.

Opening assault • *Animation development (above); final render (right)* • Each image shows the progress of one particular frame in a single shot in the Energy Facility sequence. 1. Previsualization work is mapped out by the layout team to establish the general flow of action in a complicated shot; 2. Animation of the airplane is tracked in a slightly higher resolution render. Effects work for explosions and smoke plumes is laid into the shot; 3. Final composited render expresses the full-blown action and atmosphere in the shot.

"It was important to get this scene right as it sets the tone for everything that follows. Striking a balance between the exciting propulsive action and the comedy was a challenge, but also immense fun."

David Burrows, Editor

Power lines • *Concept art, Adam Duncan* • Great energy was put into this line drawing in order to inform a complicated set build. The giant exterior statue depicts Zeus holding two neon lightning bolts. The statue was designed by Adam Duncan and constructed by Adam Ryan at Animal Logic.

LOCATIONS

ORPHANAGE

Unfortunately, Bruce Wayne isn't the only orphan in Gotham City. Luckily, the city cares about these young citizens and houses them temporarily in an Orphanage. It might not be the prettiest building, but at least it gives them a roof over their heads, a warm bed, and a hearty meal. Of course, the orphans always have each other, and occasional visits from Batman, who bestows gifts on them from his Merch Gun.

Bat merch • *Concept art, Tim Pyman and Michael Patton* • When he takes a moment out of his busy, egocentric, crime-fighting life, Batman swings by the Orphanage to douse the little ones in Bat merch. Here's what they look like after a brief but bountifully bat-logoed visit.

Gray but guarded • *Concept art, Adam Duncan* • The institution that is the Gotham City Orphanage gives the impression that it got a good deal on its real estate, since it is situated near high-tension wires, fuming factories, highway overpasses, and the neglected outskirts of the city. But how about those balloons? They really cheer a place up, right?

Brighter days ahead • *Concept art, Thomas Zenteno* • The art department illustrates key moments during pre-production that help establish the mood of the movie. This visual-development image of the Orphanage dorm shows a light space, suggesting a bright future for the orphans.

"Our approach to the look of the film was full of contradictions. We wanted the film to look dark and moody yet full of light and color."

Grant Freckelton, Production Designer

ARKHAM ASYLUM

Located on the outskirts of Gotham City, Arkham Asylum was established in the DC Universe in 1974 and named after a town in American author H.P. Lovecraft's horror stories. The purpose of this building is to securely contain criminals in need of psychiatric treatment, namely all the Rogues that plague the city. When transplanting this maximum-security facility into the LEGO realm, concept artists visualized numerous ways in which it might be constructed.

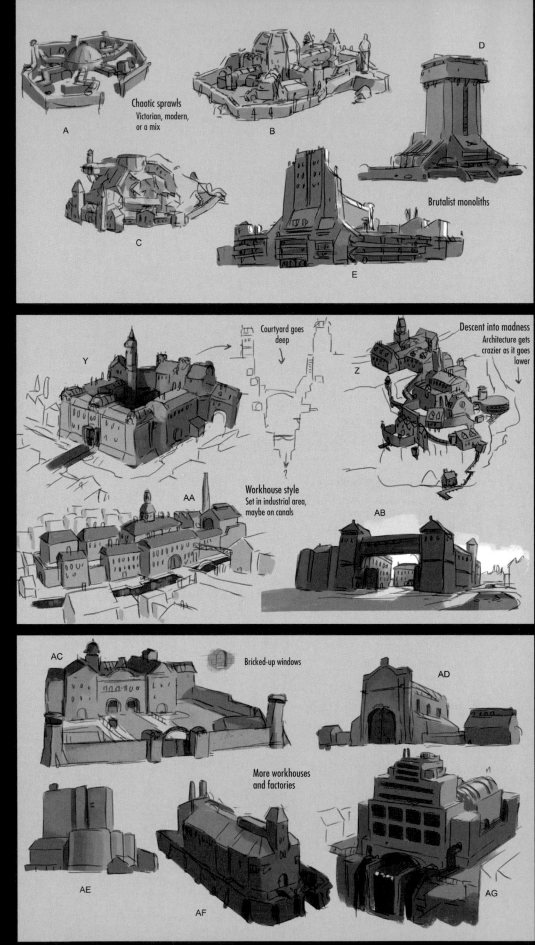

Chaotic sprawls
Victorian, modern, or a mix

A

B

C

D

Brutalist monoliths

E

Courtyard goes deep

Descent into madness
Architecture gets crazier as it goes lower

Y

Z

AA

Workhouse style
Set in industrial area, maybe on canals

AB

AC

Bricked-up windows

AD

More workhouses and factories

AE

AF

AG

Multiple design personalities • *Concept art, Adam Duncan* • From brutalist to chaotic and from fortress to workhouse, many different building styles are explored in these initial sketches of Arkham Asylum.

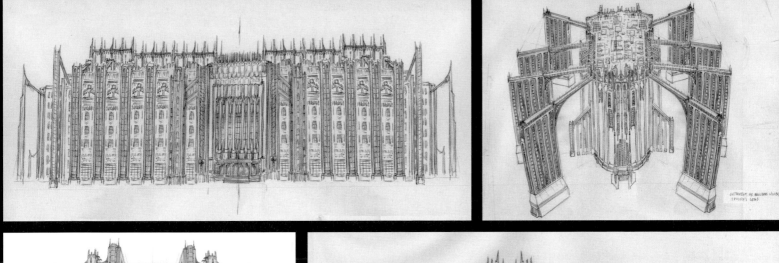

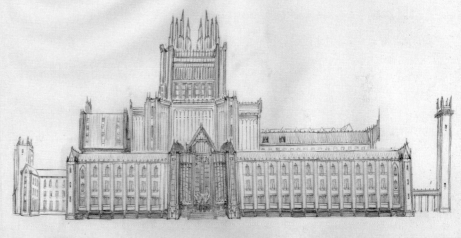

Refined confinement • *Concept art, Matt Hatton* • Pencil sketches show diverse concepts for Arkham Asylum in great detail, some influenced by famous prisons in films such as *The Green Mile* (1999).

Island living • *Concept art, Adam Duncan* • Inspired by the legendary Alcatraz Federal Penitentiary off the coast of San Francisco, Arkham Asylum is a far cry from an island paradise. The shape and layout is established in this environment drawing.

Enter here • *Concept art (top and middle), Adam Duncan; animation development (bottom)* • Exploration of the Arkham Asylum entryway in both brutalist and Gothic looks raised questions as to whether the proposed metal-wrought lettering would be possible to build in LEGO bricks. The bottom image shows the built version.

STOP
SECURITY
SCREENING
PART 1

NO CHROME
PIECES
NO CAKES
NO SHARP
EDGES

A view from inside • *Animation development* • This tour of Arkham Asylum provides a detailed look at important prison locations. Thoughtfully, each has been shown with the wear and tear that a real-world prison setting might be expected to exhibit, but a LEGO build typically would not.

Dinner time • *Concept art, Adam Duncan* • The captive Rogues do not
look pleased to be eating together in the prison cafeteria. Only the
Joker has retained his trademark smile while doing hard time.

"The cafeteria space inhabited by the Rogues is part of an underground 'Super Duper Max Facility,' a high-tech mixture of a prison and hospital meant to keep the most challenging villains locked up."

Penned up • *Concept art, Adam Duncan* • Which is the best way to contain the criminals at Arkham Asylum? Cells in the round or stacked, barred, and glassed? The underground portion of Arkham was later designed by Kristen Anderson, based on a round, Panopticon layout.

"We imagined a back story for Arkham, where it was built as an asylum at the turn of the last century, but as Gotham's villains became more nefarious they needed to increase the scope of the facility. Rather than expanding Arkham outwards, they built an underground facility.**"**

Grant Freckelton, Production Designer

Blocked in • *Animation development* • This design makes excellent use of the LEGO stacking system to provide the many cells required for the many inmates. Each maximum-security cell is a sealed cube, watched over by a central guard tower.

FORTRESS OF SOLITUDE

When Batman pays an unexpected visit to Superman's Fortress of Solitude, he expects to find his fellow hero alone. He actually discovers a huge party for Justice League members. This allows a fun, nostalgic reunion of characters from DC history and a chance to gather together old and new LEGO minifigures. It also serves as another reminder of Batman's isolation and loneliness.

57th Anniversary
JUSTICE LEAGUE
Party

Party banner • *Graphic art* • This bold banner design proclaims that this is the 57th Anniversary Party of the Justice League, a real-world nod to the Justice League's comic book debut in 1960. Supposedly, Batman has been invited to the last 56 parties but has never shown up.

Party, what party? • *Concept art, Adam Duncan* • Good times are shared by good friends ... but not by Batman, whose e-vite must have been delivered into his spam folder.

Chilly, crystalline wonder • *Final render* • Batman and Robin approach the Fortress of Solitude in all of its radiant, shimmering, magically lit glow.

Green Arrow	**Zan**	**Gleek**	**Jayna**	**Cyborg**	**Black Canary**

Cast of caped characters • *Concept art, Vivienne To and Tim Pyman* • Party attendees included lesser-known Justice League members as well as their more famous teammates.

PHANTOM ZONE

Originating in Superman lore, the Phantom Zone is an inescapable prison for the worst villains in the universe. It exists in another dimension and only the Man of Steel possesses the projector transportation technology to move prisoners in and out. The Phantom Zone of THE LEGO BATMAN MOVIE shares this unique dimensionality.

" ... impossible shape and form, limitless and never-ending, with infinite details. "

Miles Green, Effects Supervisor

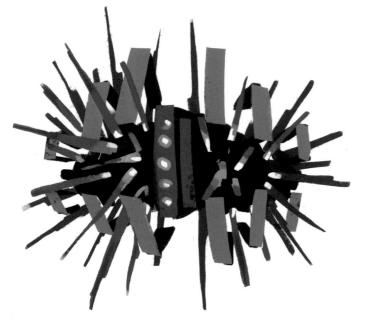

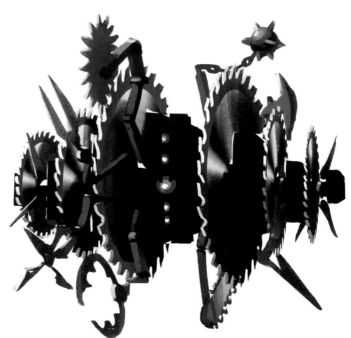

Watchful figure • *Concept art, Adam Duncan* • An early idea for the Phantom Zone was to staff it with a mysterious Phantom Zone Guard—a Kryptonian Guard Robot from the Fortress of Solitude supplied by Superman to keep a digital eye on prisoners. If any villains tried to escape, the Guard could deploy this threatening defense mode.

Message from beyond • *Concept art, Noemie Cauvin* • Colorscript images show a nebulous cyan and magenta color palette, partly inspired by depictions of the Phantom Zone in other media. Green lightning was added in the scenes where the Joker has control of the Zone, to reflect his purple and green colors.

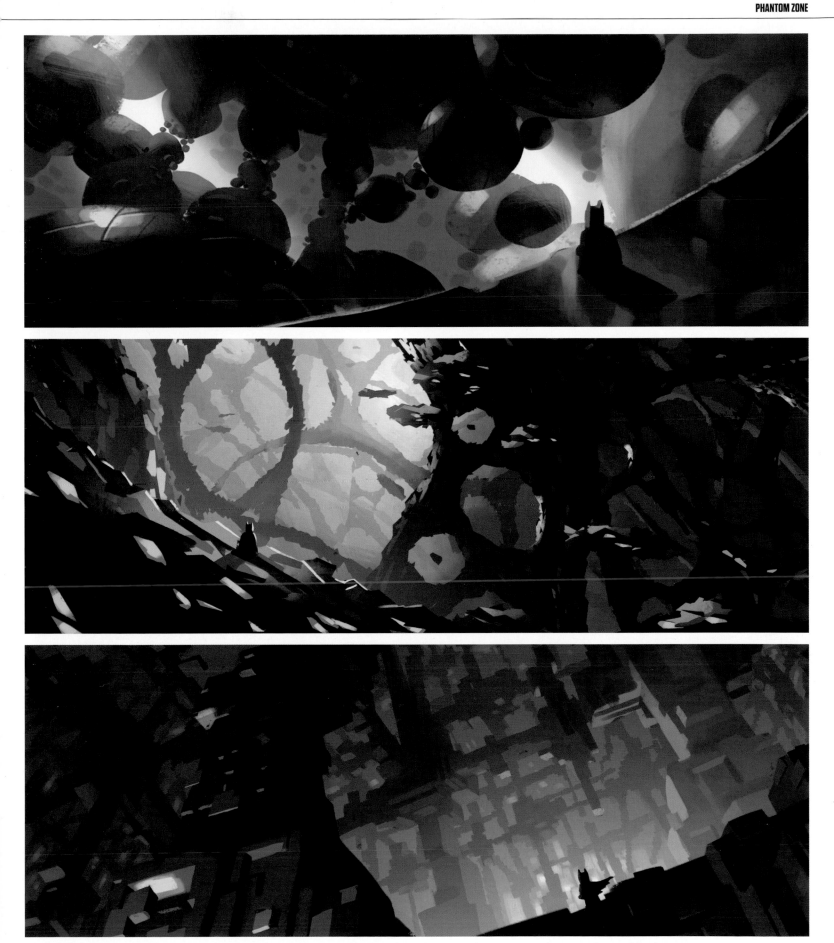

Never-ending chaos • *Concept art, Adam Duncan* • In these concept images, scale, color, and motion explorations present the great unknown of the Phantom Zone, dwarfing Batman with its massive construction, or rather deconstruction. Shapes vary from rounded, organic forms to more traditional LEGO squared structures, the whole projecting a strange and unsettling environment.

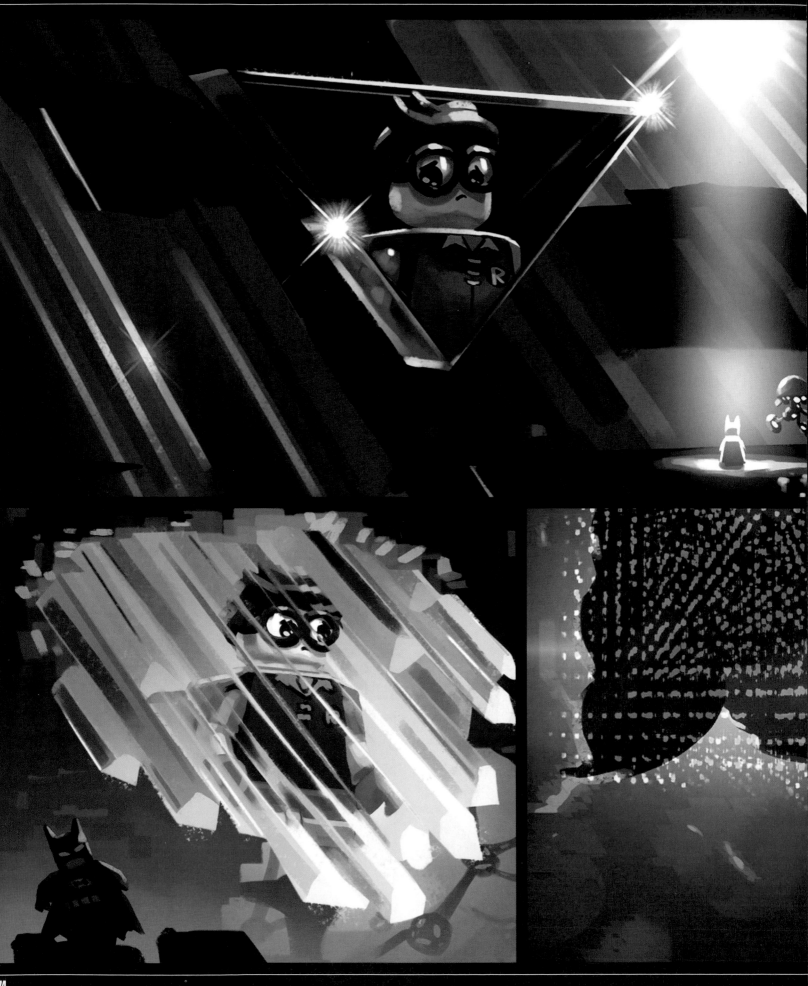

Young man in the mirror • *Concept art, Adam Duncan* • Phantom Zone concept art presents the ways in which the imprisoned Batman might watch the action in Gotham City through the dimensions separating them. Images here reflect elements from Superman's history, with crystal structures and cool, icy blues that are reminiscent of Krypton.

CHARACTERS

BATMAN

"I'm Batman." It's a big name for a small-scale Super Hero to live up to. But Batman knows he is a legend, after all he is a combination of more than 75 years of DC Comics history and 65 years of LEGO® creativity. No wonder this diminutive yet dynamic Super Hero has more ego than his cape and cowl can contain.

Man of action • *Concept art, Lianne Hughes* • These character pose designs and story sketches are partly inspired by previous Batman incarnations. They show Batman in many situations, from performing daring stunts to signing autographs and taking selfies.

Stunned (wide-eyed)

Angry (deeply furrowed brow)

Sad (upturned brow)

Confused (wide-eyed, eyebrow raised)

Smug (eyebrow raised, grin)

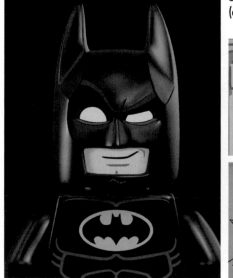

Disappointed (furrowed brow)

Man behind the mask • *Concept art, Tim Pyman, Simon Ashton, Scott Hurney, Emily Dean, Chris Paluszek, David Tuber, and Yori Mochizuki* • Batman is a man of emotion and expression, even with a cowl covering most of his face. This selection of facial and cowl shapes was sketched and animated by the character design team.

Letting his cape down • *Concept art (above), Vivienne To; final render (right)* • Ready to chill out after a tough day fighting crime, Batman wears a designer silk robe that suits his billionaire lifestyle. The designer first worked through the color concept to find a luxury look, then found the perfect pattern to complement Batman's painted-on pecs and abs.

Robed and ready to relax • *Final render* • Batman dons the perfect robe from his extensive wardrobe in this final render image.

Beach bat • *Final render* • A relaxed beach look developed by the design team has the Super Hero in bat-emblazoned swim briefs. In an early concept design, he boasted bat-shaped chest hair.

Swim style • *Final render* • Batman always has the right themed merchandise to hand. The design team created a duck inflatable sporting a Batman-style eye mask to complete his less revealing swimwear look.

Building the belt • *Concept art, Vivienne To* • Batman loves his gear and gadgets, but this is the first time his iconic Utility Belt has been made as a separate LEGO element. The piece should help him catch villains even more efficiently than the printed versions that appeared on earlier minifigures did. Painted-on concept art from the movie design team helped the LEGO Group develop the final belt element.

Glam Metal Batman

Fairy Batmother

Excalibur Batman

El Murcielago

SWAT Batman

Krampus Bat

Caveman Batman

Showman Batman

Boo Batman

Military Leader Batman

Disco Batman

Clown Batman

A man for all occasions • *Concept art, Tim Pyman, Nadia Attlee, and Fiona Darwin* • Batman reveals the true joy of having a huge wardrobe in these never-before-seen Batman looks. Some of the outfits—shown here as concept art—appear in physical form in THE LEGO BATMAN MOVIE toy sets and the Collectible Minifigures line.

The Batriot

St. Batrick's

Easter Batman

Baturion

Scu-bat

Merbat

Wizbat

Racer Batman

Arctic Bat

Tartan Batman

Prom Date Batman

Batsketball Player

Rainbow is the new black • *Concept art, Thomas Zenteno* • Batman plays the role of a smooth fashionista in this rough colorscript sketch. Colorscripts are created to define the palette, light, and tone in movie sequences, and this wardrobe scene certainly brings some bright colors into the Dark Knight's world.

Batwalk fashions • *Final render* • Batman throws his own celebration ahead of Commissioner Gordon's retirement Gala: a tuxedo dress-up party for one.

Suit and cowl • *Concept art, Marie Sertillanges* • Stripes, leopard print, or dollar bills ... this array of crazy and colorful tuxes is a small selection of those conceptualized by the LEGO Group for Batman's tuxedo dress-up party.

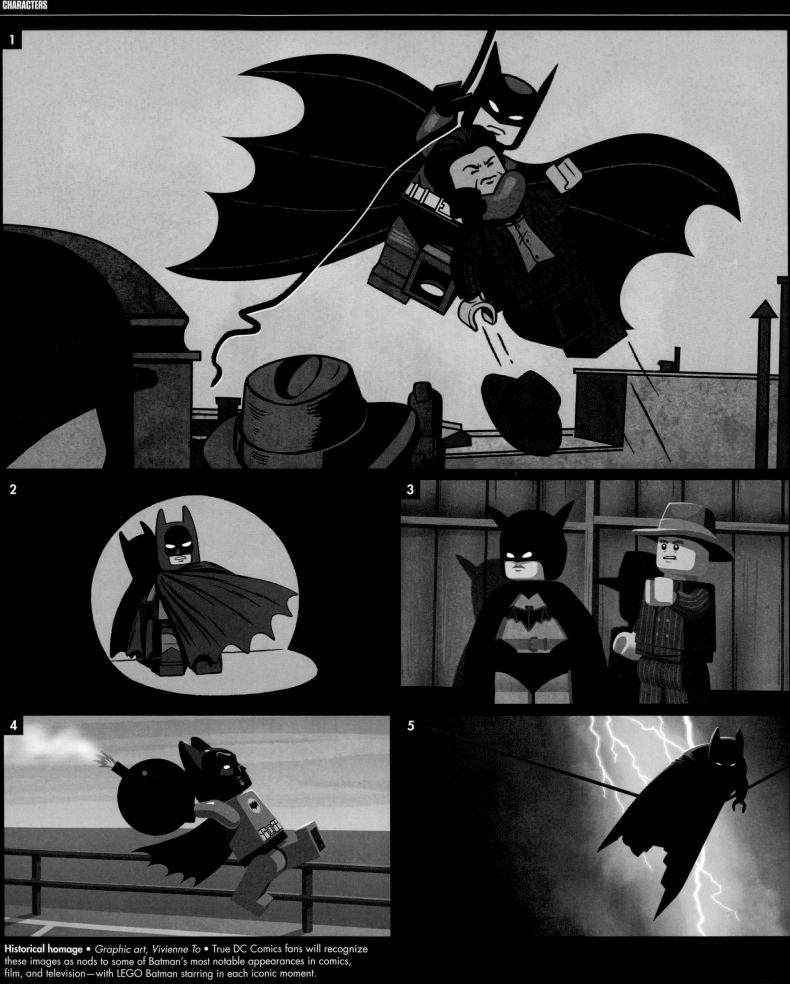

Historical homage • *Graphic art, Vivienne To •* True DC Comics fans will recognize these images as nods to some of Batman's most notable appearances in comics, film, and television—with LEGO Batman starring in each iconic moment.

6

7

8

9

10

Iconic inspiration • 1. *Detective Comics #27* (1939); 2. *Batman #9* (1942); 3. *Batman* (1943 movie, dir. Lambert Hillyer); 4. *Batman: The Movie* (1966 movie, dir. Leslie H. Martinson); 5. *The Dark Knight Returns* (1986, written by Frank Miller); 6. *Batman* (1989 movie, dir. Tim Burton); 7. *Batman: The Animated Series* (1992–1995 TV show); 8. *Batman Begins* (2005 movie, dir. Christopher Nolan); 9. *Batman v Superman: Dawn of Justice* (2016 movie, dir. Zack Snyder); 10. *Super Friends* (1973–1986 TV show).

BRUCE WAYNE

Bruce Wayne is a handsome billionaire who lives in a mansion, but he cannot find happiness just being himself. No matter how bright his million-dollar smile seems, Bruce lives with a dark emptiness in his heart—the loneliness of living without a true family. His life of luxury does give the chance for some lavish designs, though!

" As great of a life as he seems to have, Bruce Wayne is happiest when he is Batman. "

Trisha Gum, Story Supervisor

Bruce's beginnings • *Concept art, Lianne Hughes* • Early sketch exploration for Bruce reveals different options for hair and cheekbone details.

Vintage Bruce • *Concept art, Vivienne To* • Early art direction explored a distinctly 1970s look for the movie, reflected in these stylish suits for Bruce. A large collar, monogrammed jacket, chest hair, and slicked back coiffure make Bruce look ready to go from boardroom to dancefloor. Big sunglasses and a gold chain complete the look. Although Bruce's retro suits were lost, influence of 1970s style can still be seen in many of the Gotham City sets, vehicles, and background characters.

Famous faces • *Concept art, Carey Yost* • Inspiration for Bruce's expressions comes from a previous Batman, George Clooney, and LEGO Batman voice actor himself, Will Arnett.

Putting on the ritz • *Concept art, Vivienne To* • A number of tuxedo options were explored before Bruce's Gala finery was determined.

He IS Batman • *Concept art, Lianne Hughes* • Footage from Will Arnett's recording sessions was used to transfer the actor's expressions onto the animated minifigure.

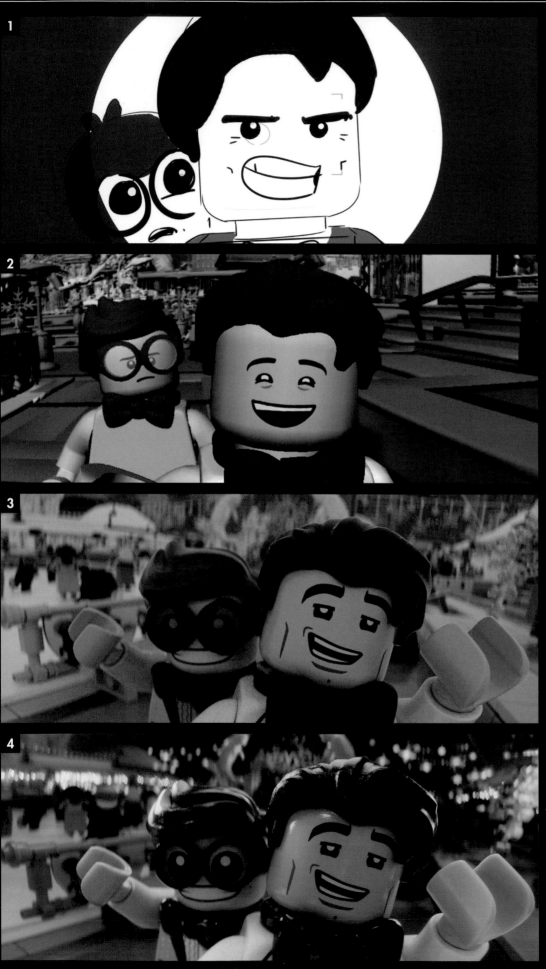

1

2

3

4

The dynamic duo in dynamic animation stages •
*Storyboard art (top), Emily Dean; animation
development (middle); final render (bottom) •*
The same frame of Dick and Bruce at the Gala
is shown in four steps of the animation pipeline:
1. Storyboard sketch maps out initial staging and
emotion; 2. Rough layout establishes the camera
angle, environmental elements, and suggested
positioning; 3. Rough animation portrays a
low-resolution version of the CG action;
4. Final render shows lighting, ambient
effects, camera focus, and, most importantly,
Dick and Bruce in high resolution.

Winter wonderland • *Animation development (top); final render (above)* • As scenes develop, the physical environment is transformed from plastic bricks to a fantastically formal affair. These two images show how a LEGO set can provide a detailed background when rendered with characters, atmosphere, and various types of lighting.

Dark Knight in the limelight • *Final render* • For a vigilante who normally prefers the shadows, Bruce is a natural in front of the flashing cameras of Gotham City's press.

ALFRED PENNYWORTH

Trusted butler Alfred Pennyworth has been an important figure in Bruce Wayne's life from the day Bruce was born. Alfred had served Thomas and Martha Wayne for years, and after their untimely deaths he took it upon himself to care for the orphaned Bruce, tending to the boy's every need. Shaped by his military background, Alfred brings myriad talents into play in his service in the Batcave. This wise aide doesn't bow to Batman's every order, but all his acts are made out of concern for his masked master.

Suitably starched • *Concept art, Nadia Attlee* • Costume explorations stuck to classic pieces for Alfred: pin-striped pants, a tailcoat, and a starched collar. The starched collar was then created as a separate LEGO element, especially for this movie.

Always on duty • *Concept art, Vivienne To* • As the sole member of Bruce Wayne's staff, Alfred is on call to complete any job, at any time of day or night. The design team created not only a chauffeur's uniform for the butler, but also some ideas for nightwear in case of a late night wake-up call.

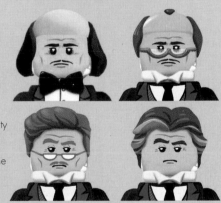

Hair today ... • *Concept art, Vivienne To* • A man of such dignity and responsibility should be crowned with just the right hair to express his age ... and perhaps the fact that working for a challenging chap like Batman causes a few gray or lost hairs along the way.

Bat butler • *Concept art, Vivienne To* • When the time came for Alfred to Batsuit up, the art department dug into the Batman archives for some suitably iconic inspiration. The gray and blue suit was inspired by Adam West's Batman costume, while the dapper black concept combines elements of a traditional Batsuit with Alfred's trademark starched collar and pocket watch. It even has a handy broom for cleaning up after Batman.

Master of the domestic domain • *Concept art, Donald Walker* • To get an early sense of Alfred's character, the design team considered the many jobs he might be responsible for around Wayne Manor, from rooftop to toilet bowl. Even with the sometimes limiting shape of LEGO minifigure hands, Alfred gets the jobs done efficiently and in top-notch style.

"Wayne Island has its own helipad, funicular rail system, equestrian facilities, marina, and croquet lawn. Alfred even has a small living quarters by the water on the other side of the island."

Grant Freckelton, Production Designer

BARBARA GORDON

Barbara Gordon has a varied history in the DC world. She has been a librarian, a congresswoman, and a computer hacker. Multiple career options were explored by the story group before her role in this film was settled: as a top cop and the ideal successor to the role of Commissioner upon her father's retirement.

"Barbara Gordon comes in with a big idea to fix the most crime-ridden city in the history of comics and literature and film."

Chris McKay, Director

Cop costumes • *Concept art, Vivienne To, Fiona Darwin, and Tim Pyman* • As Police Commissioner, Barbara needs an outfit for every eventuality. As well as uniform and plainclothes detective outfits, various designs were considered for her appearance at her father's retirement Gala. Even when dressed to impress, Barbara remains a cop underneath, as shown in costume designs featuring a detailed gown over a SWAT-style combat outfit.

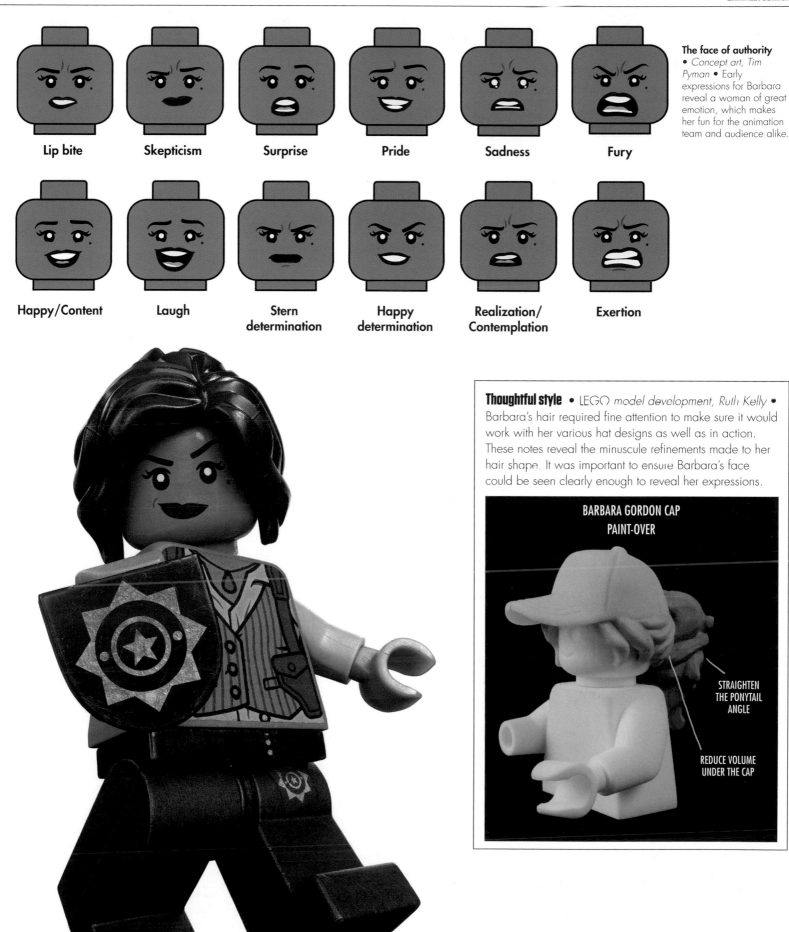

Lip bite

Skepticism

Surprise

Pride

Sadness

Fury

Happy/Content

Laugh

Stern
determination

Happy
determination

Realization/
Contemplation

Exertion

The face of authority
• *Concept art, Tim Pyman* • Early expressions for Barbara reveal a woman of great emotion, which makes her fun for the animation team and audience alike.

Thoughtful style • LEGO *model development, Ruth Kelly* • Barbara's hair required fine attention to make sure it would work with her various hat designs as well as in action. These notes reveal the minuscule refinements made to her hair shape. It was important to ensure Barbara's face could be seen clearly enough to reveal her expressions.

BARBARA GORDON CAP
PAINT-OVER

STRAIGHTEN
THE PONYTAIL
ANGLE

REDUCE VOLUME
UNDER THE CAP

ALTERNATIVE LIFESTYLES

In the final movie, Barbara Gordon embodies everything that Batman doesn't: teamwork, positivity, and working on the right side of the law. This wasn't always the case, however. Early versions of the character envisaged her as a homemade crime fighter who hid her vigilante activities behind the quiet alter ego of a Gotham City librarian.

Lover of books • *Concept art, Vivienne To* • These visuals show the casual dress Barbara might have adopted as a librarian. She may have even been a social worker at the Orphanage, if earlier versions of the story had stuck.

Rebel with a cause • *Concept art, Matt Hatton* • This colorscript depicts the proposed vigilante persona for Barbara, still watching over the city but working outside the structures of the Gotham City Police Department.

BATGIRL

Although Barbara Gordon is named Commissioner for the Gotham City Police Department in this movie, her teamwork with Batman suggests that she may one day become Batgirl herself! She dons a version of a Batgirl costume on several occasions, thanks to a blast from Batman's Merch Gun.

7A.   7B.

8A.   8B.

12.   13.

Crime fighter by day... • *Concept art, Vivienne To* • During earlier versions of the story, civilian Barbara wanted to take righting wrongs into her own hands. To that end, she may have taken on one of these tough-looking personas.

... Crime fighter by night • *Concept art, Vivienne To* • Early designs for Barbara as Batgirl show her dressed in a palette aligned with that of Batman. The two heroes have a similar silhouette, so a bright purple suit was eventually chosen for Batgirl to ensure she wouldn't be mistaken for Batman on screen.

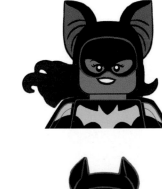

Masks and hair • *Concept art, Tim Pyman* • Initial mask and cowl options for Barbara allowed her hair to flow free, but this can restrict the performance and poseability of a minifigure character. The final design features a ponytail piece that can swing from side to side in animation.

Bad Batgirl attire • *Concept art, Tim Pyman and Vivienne To* • In an attempt to kit Barbara out as Batgirl, Batman conjured up several Bat merch costume options. Barbara looks less than impressed with these designs.

JIM GORDON

James Gordon has been an ally of Batman since the masked hero's first outing, with the characters sharing their comic-book debut in 1939. After so many years of service, the time has come in this movie for Gordon to retire from his post as top cop. The toll of working in the most crime-ridden city in the world shows on Gordon's furrowed brow!

Elemental, Gordon • *Concept art, Vivienne To* • Batman has his batarangs, but Jim Gordon might have had his own range of accessories including hats, weaponry, trench coats, and bulletproof vests, according to these costume explorations.

Dress attire to retire • *Concept art, Vivienne To; LEGO final art (far right), Paul Constantin Turcano* • Concept designs present what a true blue cop like Jim Gordon might wear to his retirement Gala. This was later reflected in the final LEGO minifigure design template.

Jim at every whim • *Concept art, Lianne Hughes* • Jim Gordon has a stressful job as Police Commissioner. He needs an extensive set of expressions to let all that emotion out.

Lasers and other lunacy • *Concept art, Thomas Zenteno* • The above colorscript image reflects the chaos in Gotham City that literally reaches into Commissioner Gordon's office, courtesy of the Rogues.

Stop those Rogues! • *Final render* • The baddies that Commissioner Gordon has spent his life chasing down are creatively featured in this render via thoughtful staging of the GCPD incident board.

DICK GRAYSON

Orphan Dick Grayson can't contain his excitement when he finds himself in the presence of Bruce Wayne, especially when Bruce accidentally agrees to adopt him. A huge, literal focus was put on Dick's childish, wide-eyed innocence, which ultimately made him the favorite character of many crew members.

Boy wonder • *Concept art, Nadia Attlee and Vivienne To* • Most early concepts suggested an older Dick than the one in the final version, with various eye shapes and hairstyles. Many were more complicated in their designs, featuring such details as a plaid shirt, jean jacket, ski cap (complete with pom-pom), and fluffy bomber hat.

"Dick is a super-positive kid who always sees the glass as half full. Really, at the end of the day, he just wants a hug."

Chris McKay, Director

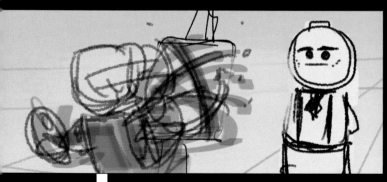

ROBIN

Dick Grayson soon steps into his own Super Hero cape. Combining the enthusiasm of youth with the joy of meeting his hero, Robin embodies more energy than a minifigure could be expected to contain. The design team enjoyed exploring some wackier costume concepts before adopting a classic look.

Caped, scarfed, and bedazzled • *Concept art, Tim Pyman* • The development of Robin's look took many fun visual turns, influenced by glittering gymnastic costumes, grungy teenage looks, and even Robin Hood.

Reggae Man inspiration • *Concept art, Vivienne To, Tim Pyman, Natalie Attlee, and Fiona Darwin* • An option that ended up in the final film is this jammin' sparkly outfit. Robin adapts a reggae-inspired Batsuit from Batman's wardrobe to create his own crime-fighting costume.

Let's get groovin' • *Final render* • One the adjustments Robin makes to the Reggae Man costume is the removal of the pants! It gives him greater flexibility for his acrobatic moves.

ANOTHER ALTER EGO

Drawing on DC Comics for inspiration, early concepts proposed showing Dick Grayson in a more mature Super Hero suit in the movie. This character adopts a muted black and blue color scheme, in contrast to Robin's bright primary colors.

How about this? • *Animation development, Adam Duncan and Nadia Attlee* • Robin tried out other Super Hero-inspired looks in a fun fashion show with Batman.

Formidable figure • *Concept art, Vivienne To* • Dick looks both frightening and frightened in this borrowed Batsuit laden with weapons.

Cowl combo • LEGO *model development, Paul Wood* • Dick Grayson's glasses posed some problems for the team when designing this cowl accessory. They had to take care that it would not impair the vision of the Super Hero sidekick. These looks consider the options, but also thoughtfully craft a cowl that is slightly askew, suggesting how a young child might dress himself.

THE JOKER

The Joker is perhaps the most well-recognized of DC Comics' many villains. He has gleefully created havoc in Gotham City for over 75 years. This film focuses on the Joker's desperate desire to be recognized as Batman's arch nemesis by Batman himself. It gives the villain a new vulnerability that is reflected in his design, as is the team's desire to create a new, fresh version of a beloved LEGO minifigure.

> "We had to create a look that allowed the Joker to be both funny and menacing when he needed to be, but wouldn't give kids nightmares!"
>
> **Matthew Ashton, LEGO Vice President of Design**

Crazy but cartoony • *Concept art, Matt Hatton* • In other media, the Joker has been portrayed with a dark edge, which doesn't suit the tone of this movie. Designers explored various looks to allow the Joker to be funny and appealing in one scene and scary and unpredictable in the next, while making sure kids would be entertained by him the whole time.

Smiling sketches • *Concept art, Sheldon Vella* • A variety of face and smile shapes were explored for the Joker in these rough concept sketches.

Colorful character • *Concept art, Charles Santoso* • Various hair and makeup colors were also considered.

The face that launched a thousand emotions • *Concept art, Vivienne To, Cara Payne, Tim Pyman, and Gibson Radsavanh* •
Of all the DC characters, the Joker offers the greatest range of emotions and the most performance freedom for animators and live actors alike.
These images show a small selection of the endless costume varieties and styles that were considered for the Joker before his final look was decided.

Fiery face-off • *Concept art, Thomas Zenteno* • In this colorscript scene, Batman and the Joker have a heated discussion about their relationship … and about the power plant that may be about to blow up.

"Our version of the Joker is in a way like Batman's black sheep brother: they fight back and forth and what they don't realize is that deep down inside they have a real relationship.**"**

Chris McKay, Director

Gaudy Gotham City • *Concept art, Adam Duncan* •
The Joker brings chaos wherever he goes, but he
also adds an undeniably fun splash of color to even
the gloomiest Gotham City spaces. This colorscript
image of a cut scene conveys the Rogue's vision
for a "Jokerized" Gotham City.

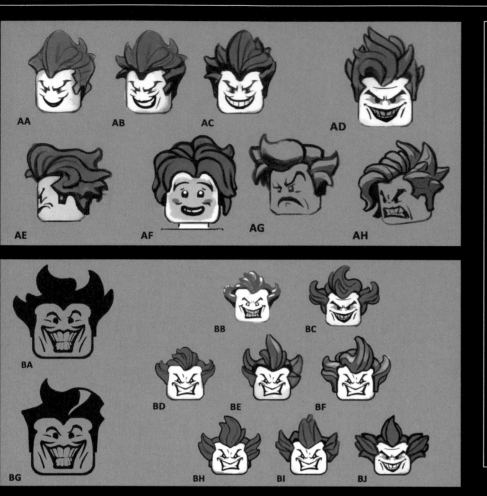

AA

AB

AC

AD

AE

AF

AG

AH

BA

BB

BC

BD

BE

BF

BG

BH

BI

BJ

Hairy scary • LEGO *model development, Gitte Thorsen* • Early model sculpts are part of the LEGO process for finessing the overall look and silhouette on a minifigure. Getting Joker's LEGO hair sculpt right was no laughing matter.

DA

DB

DC

DD

DE

TAKE ME IN

DF

EA

EB

EC

ED

EE

EF

EG

EH

EI

EJ

BATMAN?

BATMAN?

The hair up there • *Concept art, Fiona Darwin* • The Joker may not care about safety, but his hair had to be safe enough for actual LEGO playtime while also being distinctively edgy and creating a proper minifigure silhouette. Thus, many swoops, spikes, and other styles were explored.

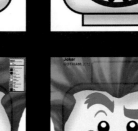

So much personality •
Concept art, Lianne Hughes •
A personality like the Joker has an infinite number of looks and attitudes, and many of these were explored in the course of his visual development for this film through expressions and makeup varieties.

HARLEY QUINN

Harley Quinn may be willing to commit crimes for her villainous love, the Joker, but she is no simple sidekick. To do justice to this fan-favorite DC character, inspiration was taken from a number of sources, making the exploration of her minifigure one of the most in-depth in the movie. Her inventive wardrobe invites creative chaos with a range of costumes, all channeling her traditional diamond-patterned look while remaining utterly unconventional.

2K Arms for Gloves Diamond Details.

Dip Dyed Hair →

Multi-colored minifigure • *Concept art, Matthew Ashton* • Notes on this early sketch point out options for "2K" or dual color molds for Harley's hair, arms, and legs.

Circus criminal • *Concept art, Charles Santoso* • Color is such an important element of Harley's look that some concept artists added color to their line sketches, bringing exciting and fun energy to her character.

Fast and furious • *Concept art, Sheldon Vella* • In the early stages of character concept work, artists sketch in quick and rough design mode to get ideas flowing and to try out different options.

"Harley was my favorite character to develop. We created a range of striking outfits for her, pairing them with a mischievous grin and coo-coo crazy spiraled pigtails"

Matthew Ashton, LEGO Vice President of Design

Wardrobe team • *Concept art, Tim Pyman and Vivienne To* • What if you crossed a punk rocker, a clown, and a roller derby skater? That's what the concept designers explored in these costume concepts for Harley. Emblematic features such as the diamond motif and red, black, and white color combination recur in many of the designs.

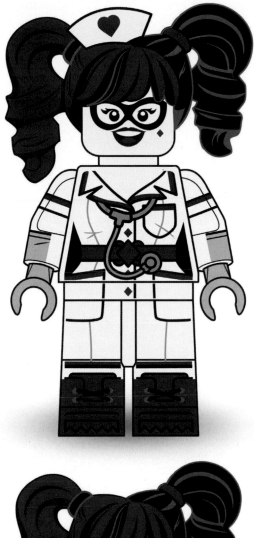

Selected styles • LEGO *final art, Paul Constantin Turcano and Michael Patton •*
These four looks for Harley—Tutu, Cannonball, Roller Derby, and Nurse—won
out as her chosen styles in the movie and in LEGO minifigure form.

TIGHT CURLS UNLEASHED!!!

From curls to cuckoo • *Concept art, Donald Walker* • A progression of concept drawings suggests how Harley's tightly wound psychiatrist alter ego Dr. Harleen Quinzel might transform into the chaotic and carefree Harley Quinn.

THEN SOMETHING LIKE THESE?

"It's great fun to take a racy DC character into the LEGO universe, interpreting her design and persona to fit into both a physical appearance and personality appropriate for minifigure existence."

Matthew Ashton, LEGO Vice President of Design

Bows and bunches • *Concept art, Tim Pyman* • Wig options for Harley Quinn take her style to new heights and widths, channeling Queen Marie Antoinette of France with some gravity-defying hairdos.

Foolish face • *Concept art, Tim Pyman* • Inspired by the facepaint of clowns and the Joker, these makeup options give Harley a doll-like style.

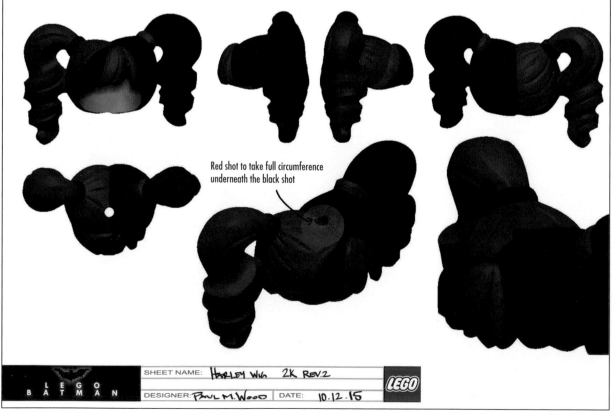

Red shot to take full circumference underneath the black shot

SHEET NAME: HARLEY WIG 2K REV.2

LEGO BATMAN

DESIGNER: PAUL M. WOOD   DATE: 10.12.15

LEGO

Hair to dye for • LEGO *model development, Paul Wood* • Corkscrew hair worked in both concept design and minifigure production for Harley Quinn. This element plan shows how advanced LEGO moldwork allows the two colors of her hair to flow into each other in her minifigure form. The term "2K" refers to having two plastic colors in one LEGO element.

DR. QUINZEL

Harley Quinn is the alter ego of Dr. Harleen Quinzel. A trained psychiatrist, Dr. Quinzel got in over her head when treating a particular patient at Arkham Asylum—that patient being the Joker. Ever since, she has lived a life of crime while still maintaining a medical practice. For this movie, many personality options for the role of Dr. Quinzel were explored in a number of entertaining ways.

Specializes in massage therapy and acupuncture, and will insist on Batman getting down to his underwear for most of these treatments. Also into spinal manipulation.

Psyche style • *Concept art, Donald Walker* • Storyboard artists imagined how Dr. Quinzel would work via a variety of personality types and practice methods, and how each would dictate her visual style. As their notes reference, practices considered include acupuncture and intensive questioning.

Tight bantu knots and extremely crazy eyes ... energetic and forward ... gets straight into the most personal questions ... nothing is off-limits ... perky.

Diverse doctors • *Concept art, Tim Pyman* • Costume design concepts were created in tandem with the story team's exploration of the different types of psychiatry that Dr. Quinzel might practice.

A doctor in the house • *Concept art, Lianne Hughes* • Dr. Quinzel listens and shares her professional opinion through the use of these expressions, as created for the animation team. Beyond the intellectual look that the eyeglasses provide, her face shapes are much more contained and reserved than those she expresses when in Harley Quinn mode.

CATWOMAN

Selina Kyle has made countless appearances in comics, television, and film, but no matter what the scenario, she always prowls along the border between good and evil as her alter ego, Catwoman. When designing an outfit for the feline fatale, there was one clear favorite—a stylish minifigure catsuit! Creators developed multiple options in Catwoman's trademark purple and black colors.

Not just the cat's pajamas • *Concept art, Fiona Darwin and Vivienne To* • Concept designs for Catwoman's costume considered various details for cowl shapes, hairstyles, and fabric colors. The final all-purple option was selected to ensure Catwoman stood out among her fellow Rogues.

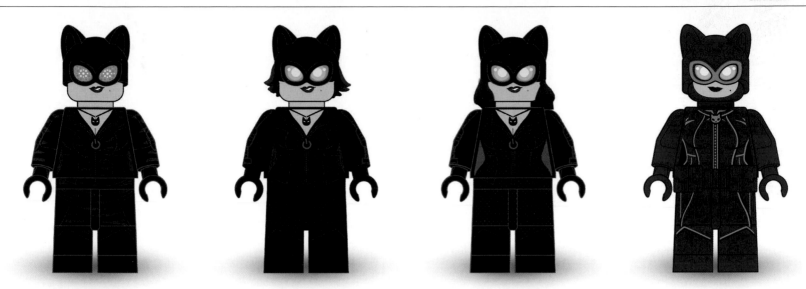

Capturing a LEGO criminal • *Concept art, Fiona Darwin and Paul Constantin Turcanu* • Designs passed back and forth between the creative teams at the LEGO Group and Animal Logic throughout development. These artworks reviewed the suit options, hairstyles, and eye designs for Catwoman.

"I'm a big fan of comics … I mean, I literally have a Catwoman tattoo on my arm."

Chris McKay, Director

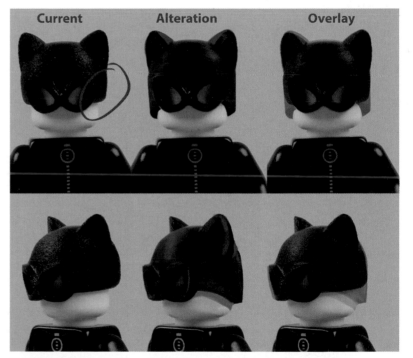

Current   Alteration   Overlay

More than one way to cowl a cat • LEGO *model development, Carsten Lind* • These visual comparisons reveal that the design teams took great care over the shape of Catwoman's cowl sculpt. They also considered how it could be reused on other minifigures. The final cowl was crafted to be a new LEGO element.

Read my lips • *Concept art, Lianne Hughes* • Much like Batman, Catwoman has half of her face masked by a cowl, so it was important to develop refined mouth shapes to allow her to emote well. The concept design team proved they could express more than just a meow, despite the cowl's limitations.

Let there be light • *Colorscript, Thomas Zenteno* • Concept art of Catwoman hacking the Energy Facility computer system in cat-like stealth mode. The character is in a dark suit and a dark setting, but a clever lighting plan allows the audience to follow her actions.

SECURITY ACCESS
ENTER PASSWORD
_

SECURITY ACCESS
ENTER PASSWORD
123_

SECURITY ACCESS
ENTER PASSWORD
ADMIN_

SECURITY ACCESS
ACCESS DENIED
_

Crack the code • *Graphic art, Nadia Attlee* • Graphics created for Catwoman's screen show her wily attempts to guess the password. (Spoiler—it's "password"!)

THE RIDDLER

Comics have long portrayed Edward Nygma as a man of great intellect, neurosis, and ego. Mr. E. Nygma certainly is hard to figure out, and proudly boasts the name of the Riddler because of his puzzling crimes. Some might say he spends too much time in his head. It's a brilliant, genius example of a head, if he does say so himself.

How many looks could one villain have?
• *Concept art, Vivienne To and Fiona Darwin* • In his movie minifigure version, the Riddler explores more mysterious fashion choices than ever before. It took many concept passes between the design teams to solve the puzzle and find just the right look for the green gangster.

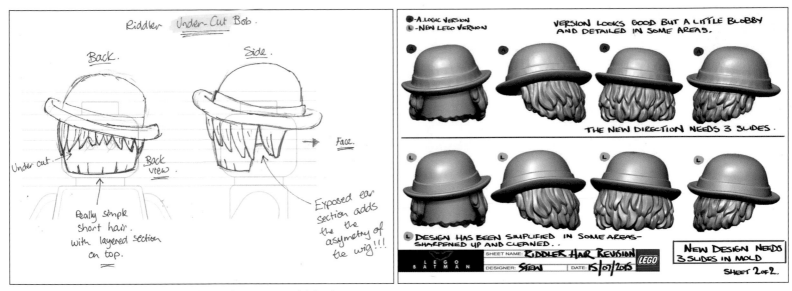

Cut to the crazy • *Concept art (above), Matthew Ashton; LEGO model development (right), Jakob Rune Nelson* • Thoughtful hairstyling for the Riddler gives a visual clue that something in (and on) his head is slightly off. The asymmetrical haircut suits the off-kilter persona of this mentally unstable minifigure.

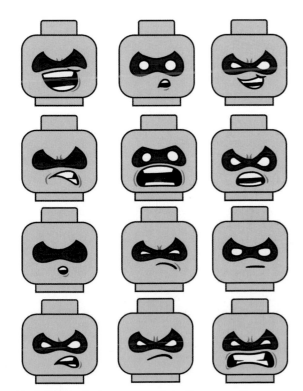

Mostly furrowed, always expressive • *Concept art, Fiona Darwin* • The Riddler is full of brain-teasing questions. To get them out of his head and into the eyes and ears of his audience, the character design team created many suitably over-the-top facial gestures and mouth shapes for him.

THE PENGUIN

Oswald Chesterfield Cobblepot is notoriously short in stature, but this mini minifigure makes up for it with a tall top hat and big ideas. Having been mocked for his physical appearance from his youth, the Penguin tries to earn respect as a wealthy businessman who conducts his affairs on the wrong side of the law. The one thing that is always in order is this dapper chap's stylish suit.

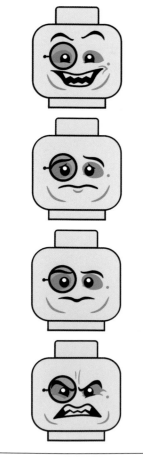

Frosty faced • *Concept art, Michael Patton and Gibson Radsavanh* • Once it was decided that this minifigure's skin tone should be an icy blue, chilling expressions were created for the monocled Penguin.

Dapper designs • *Concept art, Vivienne To and Fiona Darwin* • Concepts for the Penguin's costume design show options with various tuxedo details, neckwear styles, and monocle colors for this mainly monochromatic minifigure.

Topped off • *LEGO model development, Gitte Thorsen* • Turnaround images of the LEGO element sculpts for Penguin's scarf and hat give a sense of their proportions all the way around his head. Viewing the element at several angles determines whether or not such large accessories will hamper his animation performance.

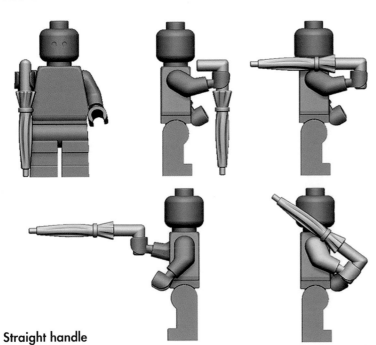

Crime, rain or shine • LEGO *model development, Paul Wood* • The Penguin's umbrella is useful for more than just a rainy day: he can also use it as a weapon. Its design involves careful consideration of how the umbrella might be held and how its silhouette appears when utilized, from every angle.

Rounded handle

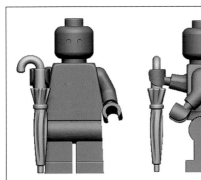

Straight handle

POISON IVY

Botanist Pamela Isley always had a deep connection with plant life, long before a laboratory accident gave her eco-based superpowers. As well as the ability to render foes unconscious with her kiss, Poison Ivy can control plants to trap them. The LEGO medium allows this DC super-villain to unleash her powers in a highly imaginative, visual way.

Vine-wielding vamp • *Concept art, Matthew Ashton* • Concept designs portray the twists and curves of plant growth both on Poison Ivy's costume and in her hair. The victory rolls in her hairstyle are reminiscent of roses, continuing the floral theme.

Glorious in green • *Concept art, Tim Pyman* • The character design team suggested a variety of hairstyle, makeup, and costuming options for Poison Ivy. Finding the right balance between fabulous details and simple readability is an artistic skill required to make LEGO minifigures suitable for both onscreen and toy production considerations. The final look for Poison Ivy was created by Vivienne To at Animal Logic.

Overgrowth in motion • *Animation development, Tim Pyman* • Poison Ivy's vines can take over an entire room in just a few frames of animation. Through the use of stop-motion-like camerawork, they grow piece by piece, reaching out to capture her intended victims.

Soft sculpt, soft curls • LEGO *model development, Gitte Thorsen and Paul Constantin Turcanu* • LEGO mold turnarounds (left) show Poison Ivy's work-in-progress hairpiece. Hand-sculpting elements is a traditional LEGO technique and, despite new digital methods, is still used for intricate design work. The final LEGO hairpiece (bottom left) shows that molded flowers and printed leaf details were later added to Poison Ivy's hairpiece.

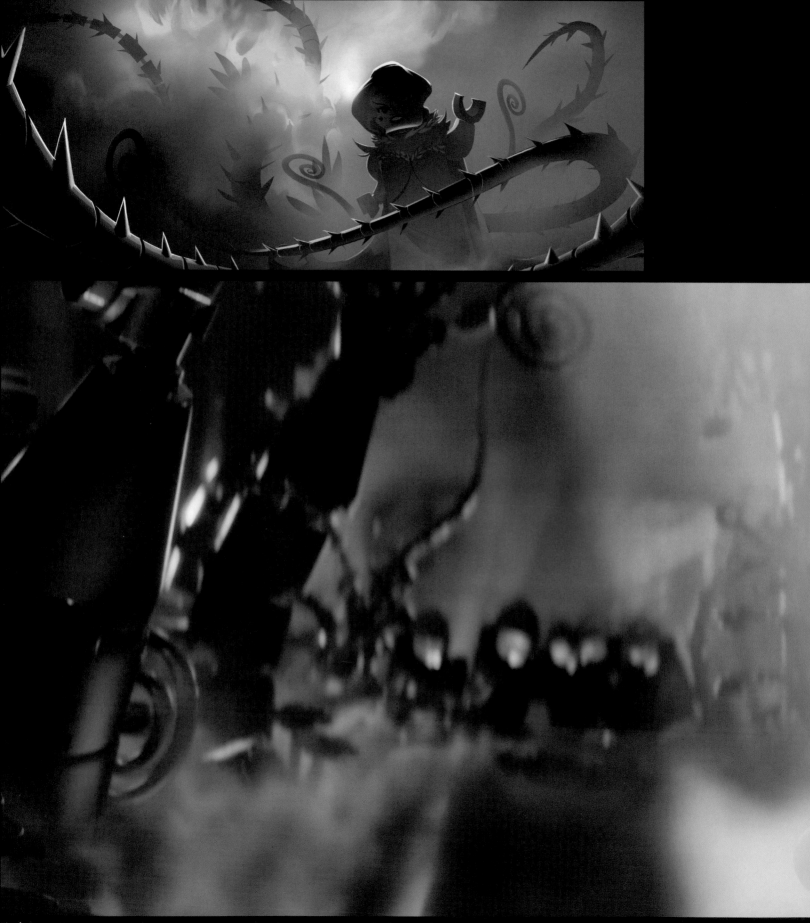

Final vines • *Concept art (top), Thomas Zenteno; final render (above)* • Poison Ivy makes her way through the
Gotham City Energy Facility, helping the Rogues to take over the power plant using plant powers of her own.

TWO-FACE

Two-Face is the rogue personality of a Gotham City attorney, Harvey Dent, turned to the dark side … or half-turned, after being half-doused with acid. Two-Face's costuming options allow more creativity than for an everyday lawyer, with his split personality and obsession with duality being reflected in some unusual suit stylings.

" I really loved the Billy Dee Williams portrayal of Harvey Dent, and this is how I would have imagined his version of Two-Face to look. **"**

Chris McKay, Director

Two faces, many looks • *Concept art, Fiona Darwin* • Various design concepts were explored for Two-Face, paying respect to his various appearances in comics, film, and television since the 1940s. The team eventually decided to rethink Two-Face's classic look of standing-on-end hair. Instead, they created a hair piece that looked like his plastic wig had melted and dribbled down the side of his head.

2K SPLIT

SHEET NAME: TWOFACE WIG

LEGO
BATMAN

DESIGNER: Nick Whitmore   DATE: 22/10/15

LEGO

2ND SHOT   1ST SHOT

Double the hair, double the fun • *LEGO model development, Nicholas Whitmore* •
With one of the most complicated toupees ever crafted, Two-Face sports a rare
mold split in his wig. The LEGO design team create these images as part of their
specification brief to show the minifigure production team where the mold split
will be and how the two differently colored pieces will be attached.

"Oo"   "Uh"

"L"   "A"

"Th"   "Ee"

Read my two pairs of lips • *Concept art,
Tim Pyman* • Mouth shapes give the
animation team a visual alphabet when
matching action to the voice recordings.

SCARECROW

Professor Jonathan Crane turned his brain into figurative straw after he conducted one too many experiments on himself. According to DC lore, he also boasts a background in biochemistry that inspired him to create his own "fear gas," to be used on victims to induce scary visions. Early designs featured raggedy robes and sewn sections to make a suitably scruffy Scarecrow outfit.

> "Some of Scarecrow's initial artwork was a little monstrous, so we simplified his sack face to make him less scary."
>
> **Matthew Ashton, LEGO Vice President of Design**

Outstanding in his field … of costumes • *Concept art, Fiona Darwin and Vivienne To* • Concept designs exhibit the various ways of creating a Scarecrow scary enough to frighten the Dark Knight himself.

Sewn but not silent • *Concept art, Michael Patton* • Scarecrow may have a stitched-up mouth, but he is still able to express himself using a variety of facial shapes and changeable eye colors.

Pizza delivery • *Concept Art, Vivienne To* • When the pizza guy is Scarecrow in disguise, you can bet his topping of choice is a blast of fear gas instead of pepperoni. His minifigure dons a Luigi's t-shirt and a helmet when breaking and entering. Even crooks with no moral qualms know that safety always comes first!

Scarecrow in share circle • *Concept art, Thomas Zenteno, Nora Johnson, and Emily Dean* •
This colorscript image shows the imprisoned Rogues wearing Arkham Asylum's finery,
including a unique uniform hat in prison orange for the Scarecrow.

KILLER CROC

Born with a reptilian appearance, wrestler Waylon Jones was pushed into criminal life after suffering years of mocking comments. Genetic experimentation added to both his beastly look and superhuman strength. As this chomping character's scale demanded, he was created in "big fig." format. Now, Killer Croc looms over the other Rogues with his huge claws and jaws.

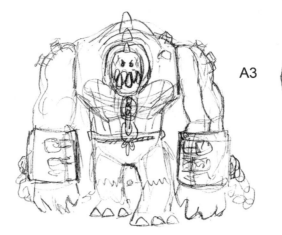

A3

A7

Sketchy character • *Concept art, Fiona Darwin* • Early concept drawings reveal very different approaches to Killer Croc's look, particularly in his head shape.

Getting to the point(s) • *Concept art, Fiona Darwin* • A vast range of variations in head shape, jaw proportions, spikes, and exterior accessories continued all the way through color concept designs for Killer Croc.

Classic croc • *Concept art (top), Fiona Darwin; existing LEGO model (above)* • After considering numerous head shapes and designs for Killer Croc, the LEGO design team decided to give him an existing crocodile head piece to give him a more classic LEGO brand look.

C12

> "Killer Croc underwent an extreme makeover compared to his previous iterations. This "big figure" contains at least seven new elements."
>
> **Matthew Ashton, LEGO Vice President of Design**

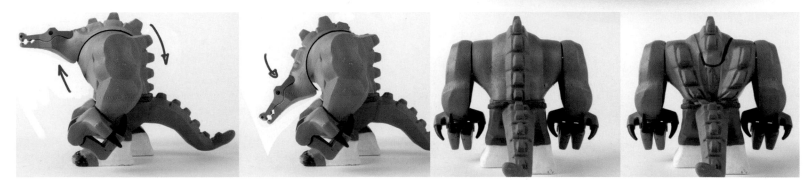

A head above the rest • *LEGO model development, Stewart Whitehead* • The red markings show the movement that the Animal Logic team hoped to get out of Killer Croc, to give this not-so-gentle giant more range of motion in battle scenes and also allow him to take a dip and go for a swim in the movie.

MR. FREEZE

Victor Fries was once a warm-hearted human with an expertise in cryogenics. The classic DC villain had already existed as a LEGO minifigure, but this movie model is his first appearance in a LEGO exosuit. When his red eyes begin to glow under that plastic dome, danger levels spike to new highs—unlike any nearby thermometers.

> "Mr. Freeze was one of the first models I started building because he is both a key character and a mech, requiring extra time to address all production concerns."

Michael Fuller, LEGO Senior Design Manager

Arcticly aglow • *Concept art, Grant Freckelton* • This art concept piece, which shows Mr. Freeze with a black head at this point in his development, gives a sense of his "glowing yet grim" factor. Evil light radiates from his eyes and exosuit.

Dome of doom • *Concept art, Michael Patton* • LEGO designers took the time to develop a full minifigure design for Mr. Freeze, even though he was unlikely to appear outside his mechanical suit in the movie. His armor and domed helmet piece is also used on the movie's Red Hood minifigure.

Built for below zero • LEGO *model development, Michael Fuller; concept art, Tim Pyman* • Early concepts of Mr. Freeze featured various armor builds, head colors, and even teddy bear slippers to keep his little robotic toes warm. Michael Fuller built a prototype model from this, to begin the revisions process.

Cold shot • LEGO *model development, Michael Fuller* • The design options explored for Mr. Freeze's Freeze Blaster show how just a handful of small bricks can make a variety of inventive, frost-fueled weapons.

Stone-cold Rogue • *Final render* • Mr. Freeze is about to lay down the cold, hard facts of villainy on a Gotham City Energy Facility worker in this final render.

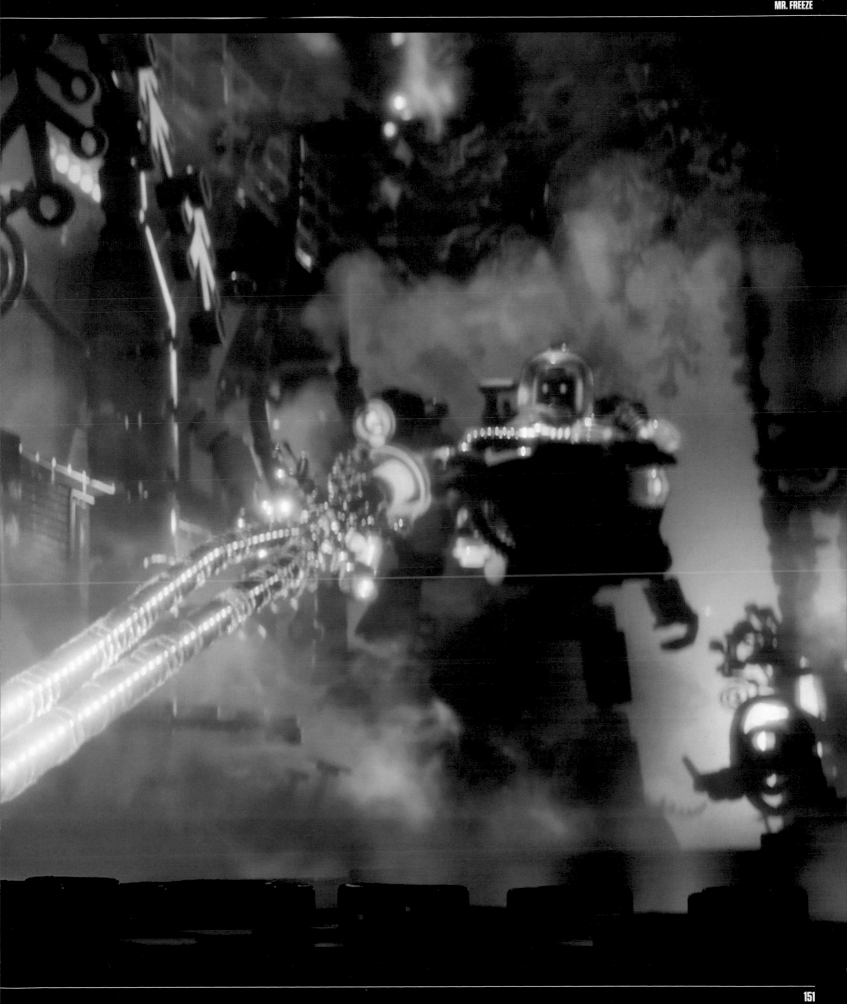

BANE

Bane is man of great physical strength and well-honed tactical fighting skills, made all the more powerful because of the "venom" formula he carries in his backpack. In the LEGO world, Bane required a "big fig." design. A minifigure would simply not do justice to this oversized adversary.

Roughed-out tough guy • *Concept art, Fiona Darwin* • Early sketches of Bane focused on silhouette and scale more than costume considerations.

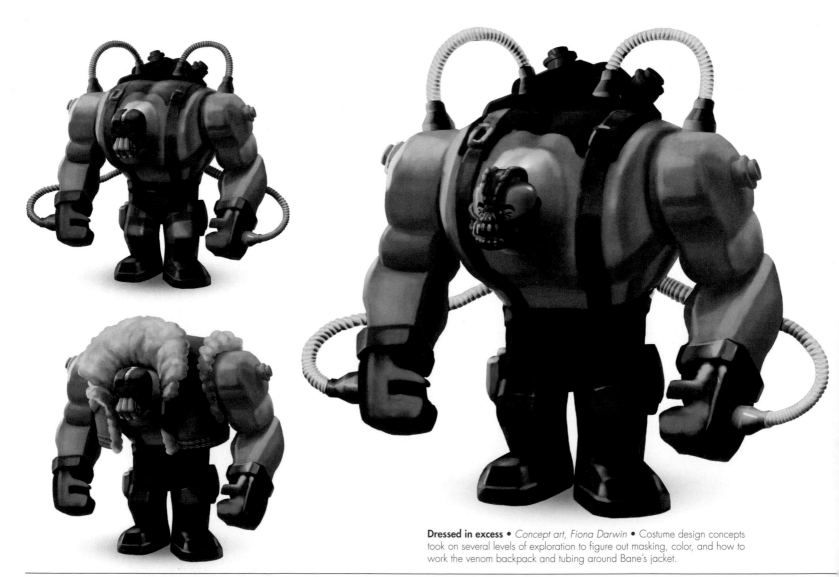

Dressed in excess • *Concept art, Fiona Darwin* • Costume design concepts took on several levels of exploration to figure out masking, color, and how to work the venom backpack and tubing around Bane's jacket.

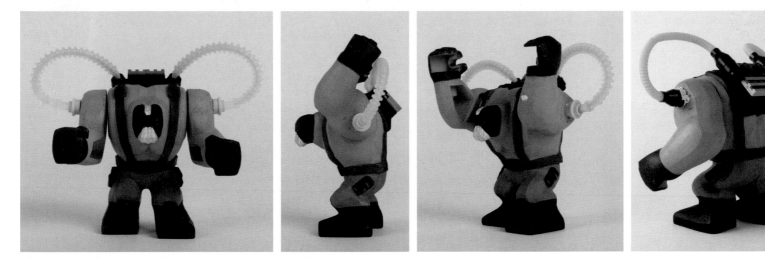

Tubed turnaround • LEGO *model development, Stewart Whitehead* • Bane's new shape required extensive development work, for both character design and product design considerations. How the elements attach to his body was a concern, as was what his body would look like when they are removed. Assessing the figure from multiple angles helped the designers make informed decisions on these issues.

"Early animation had suggested that Bane move with a five-stud gait, but since the LEGO system works better in even numbers, his walk cycle had to be adjusted to run four or six studs wide."

Matthew Ashton, LEGO Vice President of Design

CLAYFACE

A good villain is a master of many disguises. Clayface oozes into his own interpretation of that concept by shape-shifting to fight in whatever situation he encounters. He's so amorphous that DC lore doesn't pin him down to an exact human persona, and the LEGO system perfectly enhances his ability to rebuild himself into any creepy thing imaginable.

Mudtastic menace • *Concept art, Fiona Darwin and Vivienne To* • Clayface has a recognizable default form, which concept artists brick-sculpted to perfection using common LEGO pieces in a fluid manner. The look of the final animation for Clayface, as well as his LEGO model, retained the feel of the original concept art throughout the development process. The model was, however, reworked to create a legitimate LEGO build structure.

> " Clayface is the coolest character to create, and he's foolishly fun to watch; there's something surreal and special about taking static, hard 'plastic' LEGO bricks and making them look like wet, droopy, dripping mud. "

Jeff Driver, Modeling Lead

Clay thrower • LEGO *model development, Michael Fuller and Joseph Coleman* • Special effects in the movie allow Clayface to throw a lot of LEGO clay. To replicate the effect, the LEGO design team developed "Gatling guns" (or clay shooters) for Clayface's arms.

Eye-catching emotion • *Concept art, Vivienne To* • Concept artists and the LEGO Group explored many eye shapes and designs for Clayface, including some rounded and triangular shapes. The animation team later used a combination of stop-motion style animation and animated decals to allow Clayface's eyes to emote in the movie.

Clay breath • *Final render* • When Clayface attack the Gotham City Energy Facility, its workers are confronted with his LEGO teeth, tongue, and tonsils! This final render captures Clayface's large, droopy mouth—another distinctive feature that helps the character to emote on screen.

Tubular threat • *Animation development* • Rough animation portrays the arc of motion and silhouette that Clayface follows as he grabs an innocent bystander. A complicated rig inside this seemingly simple model render allows Clayface to easily change shape.

Beware the flying clay • *Animation development* • Animation combined with visual effects work shows how Clayface will release clay pods as he swirls around in battle.

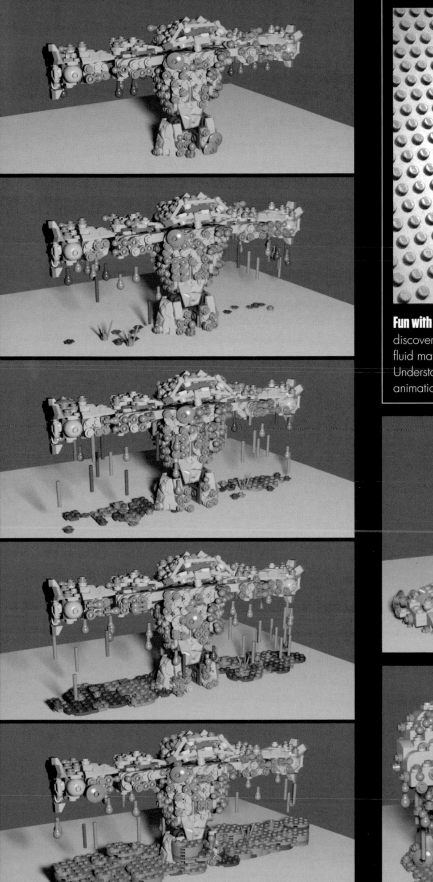

Fun with slime • *Video screenshot* • The visual effects team wanted to discover how LEGO bricks might flow if they were based in a more fluid matter, so they whipped up a batch of slime and set them afloat. Understanding the movement of bricks in this medium inspired realistic animation for Clayface.

Rise of the phoenix, fondue-style • *Animation development* • The visual effects team developed poses for Clayface in both melting and rebuilding modes to present how solid LEGO bricks might fluidly morph in every scene.

ROGUES GALLERY

Eagle-eyed viewers will spot a number of colorful cameos among the ranks of Rogues that the Joker assembles in the movie. The filmmakers were keen to make the most of the extensive roll call of villains that Batman has battled over the years, so they mined the DC archives to find a most curious cast of shady characters and gave them a movie makeover.

Killer Moth

Gentleman Ghost

March Harriet

Catman

King Tut

Orca

Red Hood

Clock King

The Calculator

Crazy Quilt

Dr. Phosphorous

Magpie

75 years of super-villains • *Concept art, Tim Pyman and Vivienne To* • To develop so many villains, the team included concept art for characters from existing comics, TV series, and movies—aiming to cover the whole legacy of Batman storytelling.

Captain Boomerang   **Calendar Man**   **Hugo Strange**   **Polka-Dot Man**   **Zebra-Man**

Tarantula   **Kabuki Twins**   **Zodiac Master**   **Kite Man**

Egghead   **The Eraser**   **Condiment King**

Man-Bat • *Final render* • The filmmaking team loved Man-Bat's existing LEGO minifigure so much that they decided he would forego any movie makeover and appear unchanged.

"Personally, I love some of the lesser-known villains like Condiment King. Who doesn't love a bad guy who shoots ketchup and mustard?"

Rob Coleman, Animation Supervisor

VEHICLES

"Black Thunder"

ARROW →

THE BATMOBILE

Batman's most iconic vehicle is the Batmobile, and it has seen numerous remodels throughout its existence in comics, television, film, and as toys. With respect to that rich history, the Animal Logic and LEGO® teams took great care to make sure the latest version maintained its cool and interesting design sensibility while bringing a fresh new perspective that is sleek and powerful.

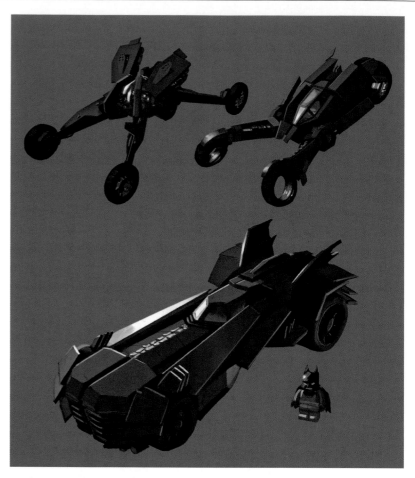

Best and battiest • *Concept art, Adam Duncan* • Film and toy designers worked together to come up with the coolest Batmobile to fight crime, both onscreen and as a real-life LEGO set.

Exploding with power • *Final render* • As this explosive final render shows, the Batmobile is put to the test in many action-packed scenes in the film.

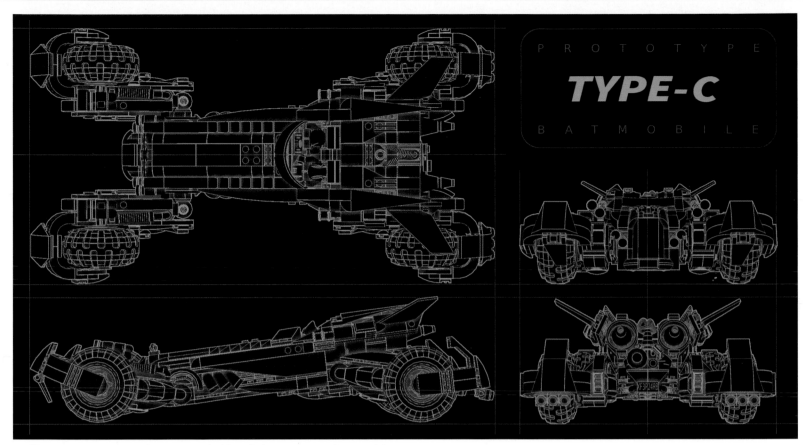

PROTOTYPE
TYPE-C
BATMOBILE

Bat blueprint • *Concept art, Adam Ryan* • To build a vehicle as intricate as the Batmobile, blueprints are a must. These detailed artworks were created for multiple Batmobile build ideas.

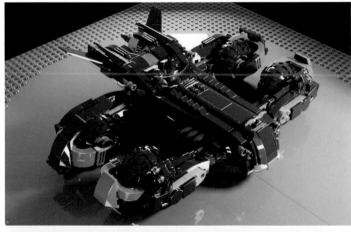

A glimpse at Glimpse • *Animation development, Adam Ryan* • The above images show the Batmobile during early concept work. Glimpse software is used to add flare and other optical effects that bring the vehicle to life.

See it, own it • LEGO *model development, Justin Ramsden, Joseph Richard Coleman, Wesley Talbott, Daire McCabe, and Michael Fuller* • The LEGO team generated numerous ideas for a new-look Batmobile before deciding on the final design. They worked closely with the studio to make sure the toy version of the Batmobile (named *The Speedwagon* in the LEGO product range) is nearly identical to that seen onscreen. It needs to deliver a dramatic cinematic experience while performing perfectly as a toy.

Taking wing • LEGO *model development, Joseph Richard Coleman* •
The LEGO team considered numerous designs for a new, aerodynamic
wing element for the Batmobile before they decided on just the right style.

> **"**It's a fine balance between retaining everything that fans love about the Batman universe, but also pushing the limits of what can exist within that world.**"**
>
> **Michael Fuller, LEGO Senior Design Manager**

Refining the front • LEGO *model development, Janko Grujic and Justin Ramsdon* • Once the overall look and shape of the Batmobile was locked down, work began on refining the details. These development images show two different but equally detailed directions.

"*The Speedwagon*"

THE ULTIMATE BATMOBILE

You can't get much cooler than a vehicle that houses another vehicle that houses another vehicle that … you get the drift. Once Batman welcomes the idea of a collaborative approach to fighting crime, he wants to equip the Batman team with the most awesome transportation ever invented, in the most imaginative medium available—thus, the Ultimate Batmobile is born.

On paper • *Concept art, Adam Duncan* • The design options and styles for a multi-vehicle Batmobile were seemingly endless, as these early sketches show.

Brick ideas • LEGO *model development, Justin Ramsden and Yi-Chien Cheng* • Once the vehicle-in-vehicle concept was proposed, the challenge the LEGO design team faced was fitting them all together! The best way of investigating and achieving this was simply to get out some bricks and start building.

In motion • *Final renders* • These final animation images show
the breakdown—or rather, brickdown—of how the Ultimate
Batmobile suits each member of Batman's team.

Automotive and aeronautic awesomeness • *Concept art, Adam Duncan •* The idea for a Russian-doll style Bat-vehicle with interchangeable modes of transportation—possibly even a horse—existed from the start of the film's development. This concept art shows an early design chock-full of power, coolness, and efficiency.

THE BATWING

Batman has owned many variations of the Batwing over the course of DC history—some leaning more toward planes, others more like rockets, and yet others more like mechanical bats. In this film, the Batwing (also known as *Black Thunder*) flies in both helicopter and plane modes, with a whole wingspan full of other exciting and surprising functions.

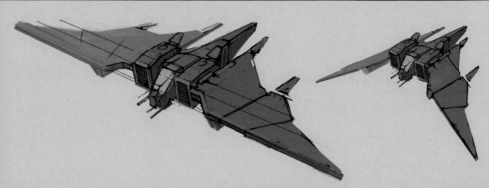

Batting ideas around • *Concept art, Adam Duncan and Jonas Norlen* • Early designs for the Batwing explored wingspan, wing movement, weaponry options, and the vehicle's overall cool factor. These sketches were created by design teams at Animal Logic and the LEGO Group.

Decal directions • *Graphic art, Paul Constantin Turcano and Nadia Attlee* • These decals, drawn by Animal Logic and then realized by LEGO designers for the Batwing toy, are used to explain and highlight various functions of the Batwing. Some of the decals were inspired by other LEGO flying machinery sets.

THE BATWING MK XII

CAUTION INTAKE

ARROW

EXHAUST

Taking wing • LEGO *model development, Bjarke Lykke Madsen* • The LEGO design team wanted to give a fresh new look to the Batwing without making the design too complex. They built in details including a new cockpit screen piece and a hidden buggy.

Booster brainstorm • LEGO *model development, Bjarke Lykke Madsen* • Attention is given to every aspect of the LEGO models that feature in the movie. Multiple options were explored for the Batwing's boosters, each using different LEGO pieces, before the final design with rotors was decided on.

THE SCUTTLER

The bat-like Scuttler is part machine, part robotic beast. Designed to easily navigate Gotham City's high-rise buildings and busy streets, it can fly, climb, jump, and (obviously) scuttle. Most importantly, it can do whatever Batman needs it to do in any Rogue chase situation.

Wings and things • *Concept art, Paul Braddock* • The Scuttler is able to perform a wide variety of maneuvers. This agility requires careful attention to its silhouette from all angles, as explored in these early concept drawings, which include a winged option.

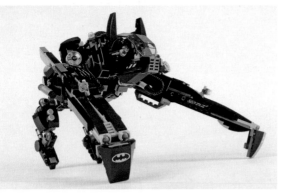

"Piloting the Scuttler would be a thrill unachievable in the real world, something we've created that only a character as extravagant and self-indulgent as Batman could ever dream up."

Michael Fuller, LEGO Senior Design Manager

Scuttler styles • LEGO *model development, Jonas Norlen* • Although the overall form and functionality were set from an early stage, exploratory designs for the Scuttler fine-tuned the model's details to optimize both the visual and mechanical elements.

BATCAVE VEHICLES

This collection of vehicles goes way beyond what the DC Comics' legacy has assigned to Batman before. LEGO bricks allow designers to create things never before seen … or driven, or sailed. All vehicles in the Batcave, whether new models or updates of previously existing vehicles, were designed to fit Batman's iconic design sensibilities, yet they drive forward a fresh new perspective for this film and its real-world LEGO sets.

Ground and sea transportation • *Concept art, Adam Duncan and Vivienne To* • The team considered mech suits, trains, subs, and more.

"You can put a bat on the front of pretty much any vehicle that's ever been made, paint it black and get something that Batman might own."

Chris McKay, Director

Vintage Batmobiles • *Concept art, Adam Duncan* • The design team placed historical Batmobiles from numerous Batman movies in the Batcave garage, from a red 1930s covertible to the tank from *The Dark Knight Returns* (2012). All of them already existed as real-world LEGO sets, so the leap to LEGO animation was easy.

Bat Chopper ("*Bat Wolf*")

Batcycle ("*Bat Hawk*")

Bat Dune Buggy

Bat Kayak

Bat-Jetski

Whirly-Bat

Batboat ("*Riptide*")

LEGO Batcave vehicles • *Final LEGO models, Janko Grujic, Michael Fuller, and Pablo Gonzalez Gonzalez* • The LEGO Group developed these secondary Bat-vehicles, which can all be seen briefly in the Batcave in the movie, as real LEGO sets.

THE JOKER'S NOTORIOUS LOWRIDER

Driven to find twisted humor in whatever he does, it seems fitting that the Joker would own a vehicle that is comparable to an amusement park on wheels. It's not all fun and games, though. The distractions the Lowrider—and the Joker's other rides—provide are often followed by a less-than-humorous end for his unfortunate victims.

Carnival of conveyances • *Concept art, Donald Walker, Tim Pyman, and Adam Duncan* • Bumper cars and a calliope cruiser were some of the more fantastic approaches to the Joker's transportation. Early concepts included a vehicle his Rogue buddies could also ride in.

Team-building • LEGO *model development, Jonas Norlen and Michael Psiaki* • LEGO designers joined together for a free-for-all "boost" building session to come up with wacky yet weapon-laden vehicles for the Joker.

Fun with the fuzz • LEGO *model development, Bjarke Lykke Madsen* • Taking the law into his own hands, the Joker patrols in a "Fun Police" car— an early idea for a Joker vehicle that was created in LEGO form during the boost session. The suspension concept was later combined with the Joker's signature style in the final model (below).

> **"** We start with a grounded design, then twist it to reflect the character's personality. **"**
>
> **Michael Fuller, LEGO Senior Design Manager**

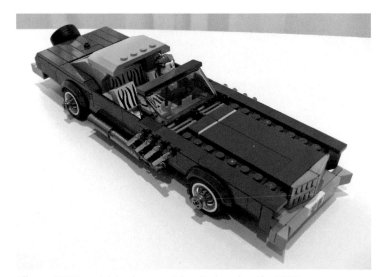

All set • LEGO *model development, Adam Grabowski* • The LEGO team had a lot fun developing the Joker's chosen lowrider vehicle for the movie. Right from the "boost" session version, the bold colors and wacky design stayed close to the original idea.

THE JOKER'S BALLOON PACK

Up, up, and away is quite a way to make an escape. This criminal-yet-creative contraption combines helium and flame-thrower power to help the Joker get a higher perspective on things.

Art in the air • *Animation development* • The design team considered a different type of LEGO balloon before deciding on a final style for the jetpack.

High-flying • *Concept art, Tim Pyman and Donald Walker* • The design team floated a few ideas out there about how the Joker might torment the fine citizens of Gotham City from above.

Out of the fire • *Concept art, Thomas Zenteno* • The balloon-bearing Joker makes a quick getaway from Batman as the Gotham City Energy Facility goes up in flames.

JOKER TRUCKS

With a personality like the Joker's for inspiration, the film's design team had a good time brainstorming all the wacky ways he might get around Gotham City, doing his mayhem-making funny business—even if they didn't all make it onto the big screen.

Comedic campers • *Concept art, Donald Walker* • The convertible options on these vehicles pay homage to classic tricks like the buzzing handshake and squirting flower, but with a more lethal punchline delivery.

Van-tastic • *Concept art, Adam Ryan* • This animated concept reflects the 1970s luxury vans that were "party on the outside, and who knows what on the inside," just the way Joker likes it.

Frighteningly funny • LEGO *model development, Marcos Bessa* • Built during a LEGO team "boost" brainstorming session, this truck design explores the idea of the ultimate clown-mobile. It gives off a creepy vibe thanks to a beastly bumper grin.

BANE'S TOXIC TRUCK

Bane is a big guy, so why not use that to have fun when designing his vehicle? Playing with scale was an important part of the exploration in figuring out the right mode of transportation for Bane, but the villain's tough-guy factor ultimately won out with a big, bad off-road vehicle.

Bitty bike to tremendous truck • *Concept art, Donald Walker* • Big guns, heavy outer shells, and vehicle sizes that emphasized Bane's hulking frame were consistent themes in the early sketches for his vehicle.

Color options • LEGO *model development, Adam Grabowski and Luis Gómez Piedrahita* • Which says mean machine better, green or blue? Neither, apparently—the winning choice is orange!

Beary nice • *Graphic art, Paul Constantin Turcanu* • The teddy bear logo on Bane's final truck is an homage to Bane's favorite childhood buddy—his stuffed bear, Osito. The toy was Bane's companion in the prison where he and his mother were being held captive.

THE CATCYCLE

Finding the purr-fect ride for Catwoman was a challenge for the design team, who had to consider a balance between stealth, power, and fun within the LEGO medium. Thankfully it took less than nine lives to build her powerful motorcycle.

Feline design • *Concept art, Donald Walker* • With many of the early vehicle considerations for Catwoman, designers had fun playing with the feline look. Some designs included simple ears or tail elements, while others explored fully feline concepts.

Racecars to robotics • LEGO *model development, John Cuppage and Frederic Andre* • The "boost" design session explored vehicle ideas for Catwoman that included four-wheeled and four-legged options.

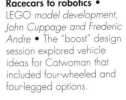

Building the top chopper • LEGO *model development, Wesley Talbott and Michael Fuller* • After it was decided that a powerful motorcycle was the way to transport this wily cat burglar, the LEGO team batted around several design options before pouncing on the best.

THE RIDDLER RACER

Riddle me this: how many ways can you translate funny business into fantasy vehicles? Apparently quite a few, as seen in these drawn and built options that the design team had fun creating. After a range of slapstick suggestions, the final design emerged as a sleek sports car.

Packing a punchline • *Concept art, Adam Duncan* • Sketch artists had a great time translating humor into moving objects, exploring why, and how, a chicken could cross the road.

Nope on the moped • LEGO *model development, Michael Fuller* • Although a moped is a fun vehicle, especially when you factor in a possible clown horn and circus-style banners, the Riddler needed a bigger ride than this little scooter could provide.

Riddling rides • LEGO *model development, Wesley Talbott, Mark John Stafford, Andrew Coghill, Michael Psiaki, and Janko Grojic •* From a dastardly double-decker bus to a question-mark-shaped helicopter, many creative concepts were considered in the LEGO "boost" building session before the final Riddler Racer (below) came to the fore.

SCARECOPTER

With its patchy, thrown-together look, Scarecrow's mode of transportation appears to have been built from a random box of LEGO bricks. The mismatched brooms on his final helicopter build are a fun touch to a minimalist machine.

Scare by air • *Concept art, Donald Walker* • Early vehicle concepts focused on flying contraptions. It made sense for Scarecrow to disperse his fear gas by air, much like a cropduster covering a field of corn with insecticide spray.

Axed alternatives • LEGO *model development, Jonas Norlen, Carl Merriam, and Nicolaas Johan Bernado Vas* • These "boost" builds offered up some complicated but fun creations that Scarecrow may have flown, as well as a more simplified suggestion that inspired the final vehicle.

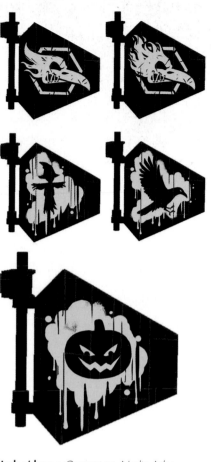

Jack-o'-logo • *Concept art, Nadia Attlee* • Various art options were considered for Scarecrow's rudder display, ranging from crows to his own silhouette. The final design is based on the LEGO pumpkin element developed for the 2015 Headless Horseman minifigure.

SPECIAL DELIVERY BIKE

Everyone loves food delivery, until they discover their take-out could take them out by emitting fear gas! As if wreaking havoc from the skies above Gotham City isn't enough, Scarecrow also gets a nimble delivery bike in the film and in LEGO set form. LEGO designer Yi-Chien Cheng developed this model from initial concept to finished product.

Pizza, anyone? • *Graphic art, Yi-Chien Cheng* • LEGO decal design once included a number to call for Scarecrow's pizza delivery business, until the team realized someone might actually call the number. Please don't call the number!

TWO-FACE'S EXCAVATOR

Although it might make for a wholly bumpy ride, Two-Face's truck is designed with two halves that reflect the duality of its owner. Both parts add up to one big construction machine that certainly looks like it can get one—if not two—jobs done with ease.

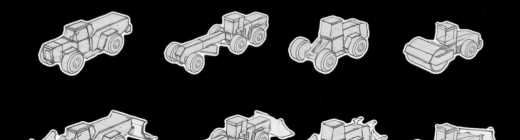

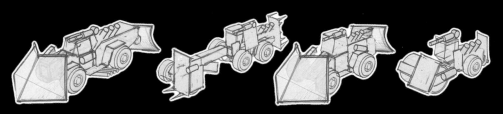

Basics to bi-machinery • *Concept art, Jonas Norlen* • Preliminary sketches started with the recognizable shapes of a steamroller or loader; more villainous details would be added later.

Double drive • *Concept art, Jonas Norlen* • Mash-up machinery was created to echo Two-Face's double-sided appearance. Designs incorporated a smooth-looking ride on one side and a spikey-looking beast on the other.

Color clashes • LEGO *model development, Samuel Johnson and Mark John Stafford* • The LEGO team explored the use of color on various vehicle options to help create two very different sides to Two-Face's vehicle.

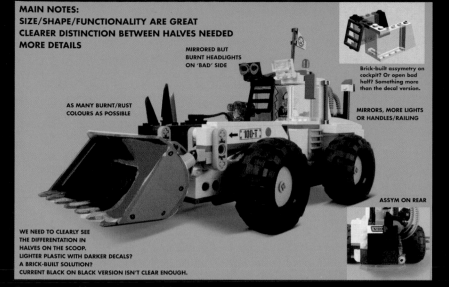

MAIN NOTES:
SIZE/SHAPE/FUNCTIONALITY ARE GREAT
CLEARER DISTINCTION BETWEEN HALVES NEEDED
MORE DETAILS

MIRRORED BUT
BURNT HEADLIGHTS
ON 'BAD' SIDE

Brick-built assymetry on
cockpit? Or open bad
half? Something more
than the decal version.

AS MANY BURNT/RUST
COLOURS AS POSSIBLE

MIRRORS, MORE LIGHTS
OR HANDLES/RAILING

ASSYM ON REAR

WE NEED TO CLEARLY SEE
THE DIFFERENTATION IN
HALVES ON THE SCOOP.
LIGHTER PLASTIC WITH DARKER DECALS?
A BRICK-BUILT SOLUTION?
CURRENT BLACK ON BLACK VERSION ISN'T CLEAR ENOUGH.

Construction critique • LEGO *model development, Janko Grujic, and model notes,
Grant Freckelton* • Despite the thousands of miles between their offices, the
Animal Logic and LEGO design teams worked closely together to craft this
vehicle, as well as every other piece of LEGO build that appears in the film.

> " Even though the LEGO team plays a big part in creating these vehicles, it's the animation team that really bring them to life, as executing the movement gives the model a whole new layer of appeal. "

Michael Fuller, LEGO Senior Design Manager

Double destruction • *Final render* • Two-Face's truck is one of the first of the Rogues' vehicles to crash and smash through the doors of the Gotham City Energy Facility, scattering bricks and frightening workers.

THE ARCTIC ROLLER

The Penguin has a variety of stylish ways to get around on land and on the water (he isn't quite so happy in the air—because, of course, penguins don't fly). Cruising around in his impressive rides gains this cold-blooded Rogue the attention he desires, which goes a long way toward compensating for his short and unimposing stature.

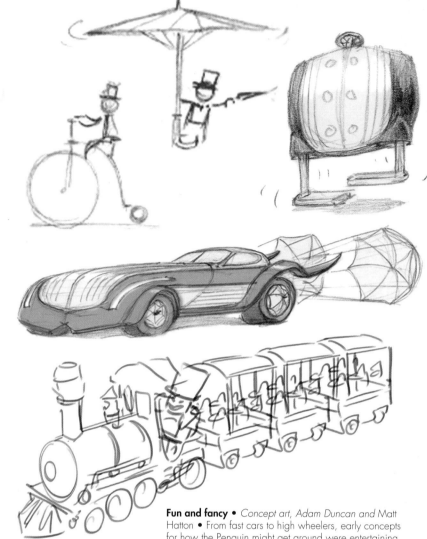

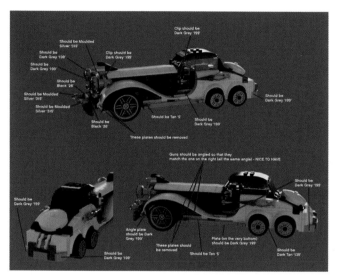

High detail on the high flyer • *Model notes* • Notes between the LEGO Group and Animal Logic designers show thoughtful attention to brick choice and other details on the Penguin's main vehicle for the film: the classic stretch car. The details ensure the vehicle is a stylish complement to the villain's formal attire.

Fun and fancy • *Concept art, Adam Duncan and* Matt Hatton • From fast cars to high wheelers, early concepts for how the Penguin might get around were entertaining and far-fetched. Imagine how cool a LEGO wind-up toy mechanical suit would have been?

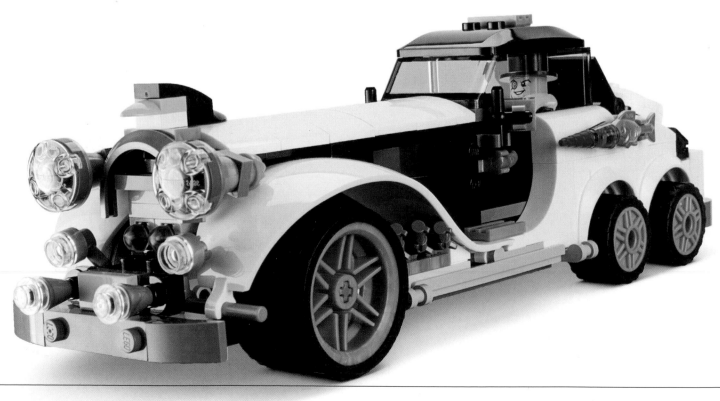

THE DUCKMOBILE AND ARMORED PENGUINS

The Penguin's Duckmobile looks fairly innocent at first glance, but it's designed to create serious chaos. Those aren't feathers, they're weapons! The Rogue's cute-looking penguin pals pack a punch, too.

Duck and cover • *Concept art, Luis Gómez Piedrahita* • This early sketch shows the film's designers considered a fire-breathing duck design for the Duckmobile before deciding to give it wing weaponry instead.

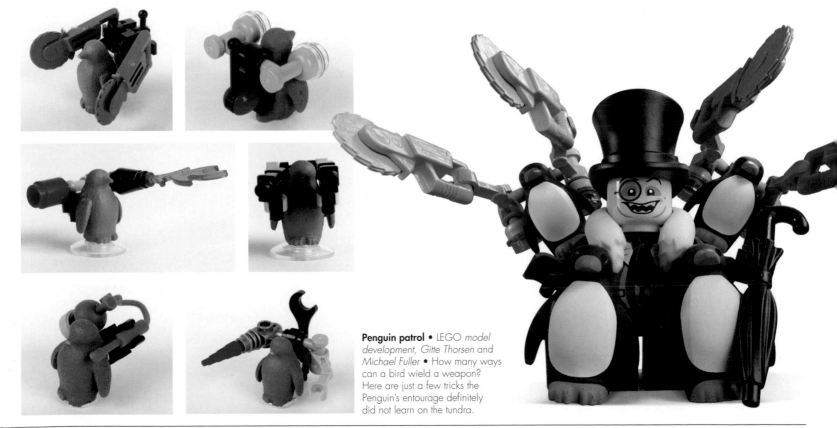

Penguin patrol • LEGO *model development, Gitte Thorsen and Michael Fuller* • How many ways can a bird wield a weapon? Here are just a few tricks the Penguin's entourage definitely did not learn on the tundra.

KILLER CROC'S TAIL-GATOR

This hulking crocodile crook had some killer vehicle options on the drawing board—perhaps the most diverse set of designs out of all of the Rogues' transportation. From swamp-worthy to circus-bound, and from mini to extra-large, his potential rides were cooler than any cold-blooded reptile.

CROC-WAGON
FROM KC'S CIRCUS DAYS. HE COULD BUST HIS ARMS OUT THE SIDES AND SKITCH HIMSELF AROUND.

KILLERCROC
"HATCHES" FROM AN EGG

FOR SOME REASON, K.C. IS A CHAUFFEUR HERE.

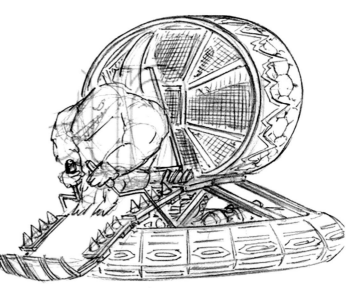

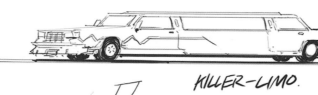

KILLER-LIMO.
WHOLE FRONT FLIPS UP. EXPOSES K.C. RIDING SHOTGUN.

Croc conveyance • *Concept art, Sheldon Vella* • Killer Croc is considerably larger than the average villain. His tremendous size meant figuring out some interesting places to put the driver's seat.

Everglades to big top • LEGO *model development, Adam Grabowski and Luis F.E. Castaneda* • The design team at the LEGO "boost" meeting came up with these renditions of a vehicle that would suit the villain's size and preferred terrain.

Swampy stickers • *Graphic art, Paul Constantin Turcanu* • Detailed designs reflect Killer Croc's rugged swamp persona. Claw marks provide a bonus intimidation factor—as if a huge crocodile barreling around in a monster truck were not frightening enough!

HARLEY QUINN'S CANNON TRUCK

Harley Quinn is a tough Rogue, ready to roll with whatever cruel missions the Joker chooses to include her in. That meant she needed a rough and ready vehicle that is equal parts rugged and armed. Of course, it must still have room for all the cruel fun that makes her the Joker's key counterpart.

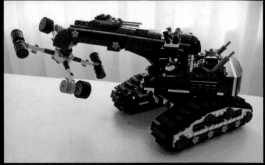

Red, black, and bricked out • LEGO *model development images, Janko Grujic, Kurt Kristiansen, and Jonas Norlen* • In the "boost" session, the LEGO team tested the road with souped-up vehicles for Harley's transportation.

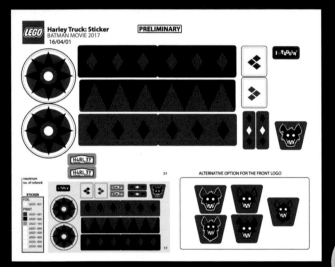

Diamonds are a girl's best graphic • *Graphic art, Marie Sertillanges* • The LEGO design team came up with fun ways to incorporate Harley's diamond motif into her truck rig, as well as her "I [heart] Puddin'" bumper sticker.

EGGHEAD'S MECH

Egghead's mechanical suit was originally conceived as one of the Penguin's gadgets, but the design team thought it would be a better fit for Egghead's personality. It's one of those "it's so crazy it might just work" ideas that the LEGO team loves. Thankfully, the film crew went along for this egg-cellent adventure.

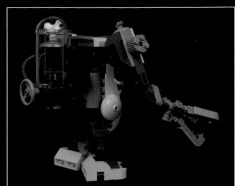

No yolk • LEGO *model development, Jonas Norlen* • Builds explored the possibility for combining battle gear with Egghead humor, right down to the chicken on the mech's back.

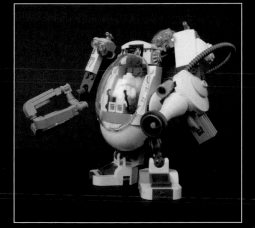

Penguin in a pod • LEGO *model development, Jonas Norlen* • This Penguin mech model inspired the designers, who put in some hard-boiled work to successfully shift it to Egghead's realm.

Eggs-pertly designed • LEGO *model development, Jonas Norlen, Michael Patton, and Paul Constantin Turcano* • The LEGO team whipped up more details than a gourmet omelet has ingredients to maximize the fun (and puns) in this mech.

AUTHOR ACKNOWLEDGMENTS

I am grateful for the opportunity to help the creative triumvirate of the LEGO Group, Warner Bros., and Animal Logic lead a behind-the-scenes tour through their collaborative process. I appreciate the filmmaking crew that somehow found time to share their knowledge with me while trying to make this ambitious movie, with special thanks going out to Chris McKay, Ryan Harris, and Samantha Nisenboim for their extra time and effort. I am always pleased when my paths cross with the awesomely genius duo of Chris Miller and Phil Lord, be it with free-falling burgers or brick-based villainy.

I was lucky to have the support of Benjamin Harper, Toby Gibson, and Ian Failes in connecting all the pieces for this project, and I am deeply appreciative for Hannah Dolan, who warmly invited me to be the tour guide on this creative adventure.

Last but not least, I am ever grateful for my own team of family and friends who are the true Super Heroes in my life, with or without a cape.

—TMZ

DK ACKNOWLEDGMENTS

DK would like to thank the many people across the globe who have provided artworks, insights, and assistance in order to make this book possible. Firstly, huge thanks to all the artists, cast and crew, and LEGO designers listed on the following page, who allowed us to interview them and use their brilliant work to build a full and informative picture of LEGO Batman's world. Special thanks to Grant Freckelton and Toby Gibson at Animal Logic, Michael Fuller and Matthew Ashton at the LEGO Group, and our Animation Consultant Ian Failes for their invaluable help and advice at every stage of the book's development. Thanks also to the following people for their roles in driving this book forward: Ben Harper, Megan Korns Russell, Melanie Swartz, Melissa Jolley, and Nick Gligor at Warner Bros.; and Robin James Pearson, Heidi K. Jensen, Randi Sørensen, Paul Hansford, Martin Leighton Lindhardt, Søren Mørup, Maria Bloksgaard Markussen, Katrine Bundgaard Holst, Jill Wilfert, Jason Cosler, Keith Malone, and Tze Hung U at the LEGO Group.

The Animal Logic team •
Photography by Madeleine Purdy

ARTIST CREDITS

AT WARNER ANIMATION GROUP AND ANIMAL LOGIC:

Artists

Laurence Andrews, Simon Ashton, Nadia Atlee, Kelly Baigent, Dudley Birch, Paul Braddock, Noemie Cauvin, Jayandera Danappal, Fiona Darwin, Emily Dean, Heiko Drengenberg, Jeff Driver, Adam Duncan, Grant Freckelton, Matt Hatton, Lianne Hughes, Scott Hurney, Nora Johnson, Yori Mochizuki, Chris Paluszek, Michael Patton, Cara Payne, Tim Pyman, Gibson Radsavanh, Chris Reccardi, Adam Ryan, Charles Santoso, Vivienne To, David Tuber, Sheldon Vella, Donald Walker, Carey Yost, Thomas Zenteno

Film cast and crew

Will Arnett, Lorne Balfe, David Burrows, Michael Cera, Rob Coleman, Alex Fry, Zach Galafianakis, Seth Grahame-Smith, Miles Green, Trisha Gum, JP Le Blanc, Phil Lord, Behzad Mansoori-Dara, Chris McKay, Chris Miller, Fabian Müller, Josh Murtack, Amber Naismith, Wayne Pashley, Jeff Renton, Bradley Sick, Jared Stern, Craig Welsh, John Whittington

AT THE LEGO GROUP:

Frederic Andre, Matthew Ashton, Marcos Bessa, Austin W. Carlson, Luis F.E. Castaneda, Yi-Chien Cheng, Andrew Coghill, Joseph Richard Coleman, John Cuppage, Jeffrey Alan Davies, Michael Fuller, Pablo Gonzalez Gonzalez, Adam Grabowski, Janko Grujic, Samuel Johnson, Sven Robin Kahl, Ruth Kelly, Kurt Kristiansen, Carsten Lind, Pola Lisowicz, Bjarke Lykke Madsen, Yoel Mazur, Daire McCabe, Carl Merriam, Jakob Rune Nielsen, Lars Roersen Nielsen, Jonas Norlen, Tom Parry, Michael Patton, Niels Milan Pedersen, Luis Gómez Piedrahita, Michael Psiaki, Justin Ramsden, Nina Buch Rasmussen, Marie Sertillanges, Mark John Stafford, Wesley Talbott, Gitte Thorsen, Paul Constantin Turcanu, Nicolaas Johan Bernardo Vas, Stewart Whitehead, Nicholas Whitmore, Paul Wood

The LEGO team • *Photography by Thomas Baunsgaard Pedersen*